Design and production by Vertebrate Publishing, Sheffield
www.v-publishing.co.uk

Wales MountainBiking

Beicio Mynydd Cymru

Written by
Tom Hutton

Wales MountainBiking
Beicio Mynydd Cymru

First published in 2009 by Vertebrate Publishing.
Reprinted with minor amendments in 2015.

ISBN 978-1-906148-13-3

Front cover photo: Steph Duits descending Telegraph Valley on the circuit of Snowdon.
Back cover photo: Looking over the Mawddach Estuary from the Cadair Idris route.

Photography by **Tom Hutton, unless otherwise credited.**

Design and production by Nathan Ryder.
www.v-graphics.co.uk

MIX
Paper from responsible sources
FSC® C016973

PLEASE GIVE WAY TO HORSES AND PEDESTRIANS.

Contents

ROUTE GRADES
▲ = EASY ▲ = MEDIUM ▲ = HARD (see page viii)

THE AUTHOR DESCENDING SNOWDON PHOTO: JOHN COEFIELD

Introduction

Wales was there at the dawning of UK mountain biking and has been pivotal in its development ever since. Not surprising really as it has all the right ingredients: high mountains, remote moors, deeply cloven valleys and of course, huge expanses of forestry. Added to which; it's also sparsely populated, meaning almost any ride offers the opportunity to 'get away from it all.'

Recent years have seen an explosion of forest trail centres, starting in Coed y Brenin and quickly developing across the principality. Whilst these offer wonderful riding, and have definitely brought visitors into areas previously overlooked by mainstream tourism, they represent only a fraction of the MTBing on offer; and anyone with a pioneering spirit and a little nous with a map and compass (or GPS) will find some far more rewarding riding on the natural trails that criss-cross the mountains and moors.

The biggest problem in compiling this book was what to leave out – there really is so much to go at. But I've tried to include a good spread of locations as well as the best of the trails.

The main honeypots are well-known: the Black Mountains are riddled with world-class tracks and trails, and loops like the Gap Road in the Brecon Beacons are dramatic enough to justify a visit to the area just for them.

The Elan Valley is perhaps the most remote area covered, and has long had a reputation for epic rides across lonely moors. But it has a gentler side too, so I've included a route here within the reach of less experienced riders.

Snowdonia's an odd one: the National Park is home to the biggest mountains and the most dramatic scenery but there are less obvious routes, particularly if you'd rather ride than carry or push. That said, Snowdon should be on everyone's wish-list; and there are many other classics too.

And then there are the outlying areas; the Berwyn Hills and the Clwydians offer some great riding; and the Gower offers one of the best trails in the whole book. And even Pembrokeshire sneaks in by way of a wonderful outing that crosses the historic and atmospheric Preseli Hills.

Finally, I know the Long Mynd isn't in Wales; but it feels like it should be, and anyway, it wouldn't be a bonus route if it was!

I've really enjoyed compiling what is effectively a book of my favourite rides, in a country that I love and have come to think of as home. I hope that anyone who rides them all will share my feelings. They'll certainly know Wales a lot better as a result.

Tom Hutton

Acknowledgements

I have ridden with so many others in Wales over the years and all of them have had an input in this book in one way or another. I'd particularly like to thank Tim Salveson for all his help and wisdom and Dafydd Davis for showing me around when much of the principality was new to me. Others like Phil Lee and Alex Cantlay have been patient models. Thanks also to *Roughrides.co.uk* for help with the Borders trails. I'd never have had so much fun without such a good bike, so thanks to Kona and Marin for their support, and also to Richard and Clare at Gateway Cycles, Abergavenny, for keeping them running. Diolch yn fawr to my football buddy, Tom Crockett, for help with the Welsh language translations, and finally, my biggest thanks of all must go to Steph for her constant companionship on and off the trail, and for her support when I'm stuck in my office for hours on end.

How to Use This Book

Mountain Biking in Wales

There's a little of everything in this book and the routes take you from stunning coastline to ancient forest and from picture postcard village to the very highest mountains. The trails are equally as varied too, from sandy singletrack to muddy motorways and from steep rocky steps to undulating Roman Roads.

Just about all of them cross remote ground at some stage though, and whilst this can be great fun, it can also be very serious when things go wrong. Don't rely solely on this book to get you out of trouble and always take a map and compass (and GPS if you have one) when you head for the hills, as well as spare food and clothes. Always keep your wits about you and ride within yourself. Most of all have fun.

The Routes

This is a guide to 20 of the best circular routes in Wales plus one in Shropshire thrown in for free. Some of the routes have shorter or longer versions available or at least some suggestions of extensions or other places to explore. It's really a showcase of most of the best bits the principality has to offer but there are many different ways of linking the best trails so feel free to experiment. Perhaps even try some of them in reverse. One thing's for sure, they are all well worth travelling for, and most you'll want to return to again and again.

Grades

Routes, climbs and descents are graded blue, red and black, in a similar system to that used at several of the trail centres around the UK.

▲ = Easy ▲ = Medium ▲ = Hard

Blue graded routes are generally shorter routes and are within reach of most MTBers, even newcomers, as well as the kind of thing you could do in a short day or when the weather's really foul. **Reds** are the kind of rides that won't actually take a full day, but you'll probably not want to do anything else once you've ridden them. And **Blacks** are those big and memorable days out that will demand endurance and some technical ability in places. These are the kind of routes to work up to.

The grades are based on average conditions - good weather and not too wet and muddy. In a drought the routes will feel easier, in the depths of winter, harder. Grades consider technicality, length, climbs, navigation, and remoteness - so one 'black' route might be a short all-out technical test while another could be a big endurance challenge with tricky navigation. As ever, these grades are subjective. How you find a particular route, downhill or climb will be dictated by your own levels of fitness and skill.

Directions & Accuracy

While every effort has been made to ensure accuracy within the directions in this guide, things change and we are unable to guarantee that every detail will be correct. Please treat stated distances as guidelines. **Please exercise caution if a direction appears at odds with the route on the ground. A comparison between direction and map should see you on the right track.**

Rights of Way

Countryside access in the UK hasn't been particularly kind to cyclists, although things are improving. We have 'right of way' on bridleways (blue arrows on signs) and byways (red arrows). However, having 'right of way' doesn't actually mean having the right of way, just that we're allowed to ride there – so give way to walkers and horse riders. We're also allowed to ride on green lanes and some unclassified roads, although the only way to determine which are legal and which aren't is to check with the local countryside authority. Obviously, cycle routes are also in.

The very understanding National Resources Wales (NRW) generally allows cyclists to use its land (again, you'll need to check with them first to be sure). You must, however, obey all signs, especially those warning of forestry operations - a fully loaded logging truck will do more than scuff your frame...

Everything else is out of bounds (unless, of course, the landowner says otherwise). Riding illegally can upset walkers (who have every right to enjoy their day) and is, in many cases, technically classed as trespass (meaning you could be prosecuted for any damage caused). Not all tracks are signed, so it's not always obvious whether that great-looking trail you want to follow is an illegal footpath or a legal bridleway. That's why it's a good idea to carry a map with you on every ride.

The Bike

Any half-decent mountain bike will be fine (try and avoid a '£99 special'). A full suspension bike will add comfort and control. A lightweight race number will make hills easier and something with a bit of travel will help on technical descents. We'd pick a compromise somewhere between the three, depending on your personal preferences.

Check everything's working – you won't be going uphill fast if your gears seize but equally you'll be a little quicker than planned if your brakes fail coming down. Pump the tyres up, check nothing's about to wear through and make sure that everything that should be tight is tight.

Essential Kit

Helmet

"The best helmet is the one that you're wearing". Make sure it fits, you're wearing it correctly and that it won't move in a crash.

Clothing

You need to get your clothing right if you want to stay comfortable on a bike, especially in bad weather. The easiest way to do this is to follow a layering system. Begin with clothing made from 'technical' synthetic or wool fabrics that will wick the sweat away from your body and then dry quickly, keeping you dry and warm. Stay away from cotton – it absorbs moisture and holds onto it. If it's chilly, an insulating layer will keep you warm, and a wind/waterproof layer on the outside protects from the elements. Layers can then be removed or added to suit the conditions. Padded shorts are more comfortable, but the amount of lycra on display is down to you. Baggy shorts, full length tights and trousers are all available to match the conditions. Set off a little on the cold side – you'll soon warm up. Don't leave the warm clothes behind though, as the weather can turn quickly.

Gloves

Gloves ward off blisters and numb hands and help keep your fingers warm. They also provide a surprising amount of protection when you come off.

Footwear

Flat pedals/clips-ins – it's your call. Make sure you can walk in the shoes and that they have sufficient tread for you to do so. Consider overshoes if it's chilly.

Other essentials

As mentioned, take any necessary spares, tools, tube and pump, spare clothes, first aid kit, food and water. Stop short of the kitchen sink, as you'll still want to be able to actually ride your bike.

You'll need something to carry this lot in. We'd suggest a hydration pack, as they allow you to drink on the move and keep excess weight off the bike.

General Safety

The ability to read a map, navigate in poor visibility and to understand weather warnings is essential. Don't head out in bad weather, unless you're confident and capable of doing so.

Some of the routes described point you at tough climbs and steep descents that can potentially be very dangerous. Too much exuberance on a steep descent in the middle of nowhere and you could be in more than a spot of bother, especially if you're alone. Consider your limitations and relative fragility.

Be self-sufficient. Carry food and water, spares, a tube and a pump. Consider a first-aid kit. Even if it's warm, the weather could turn, so take a wind/waterproof. Think about what could happen on an enforced stop. Pack lights if you could finish in the dark.

If you're riding solo, think about the seriousness of an accident – you might be without help for a very long time. Tell someone where you're going, when you'll be back and tell them once you are back. Take a mobile phone if you have one, but don't expect a signal. And **don't** call out the ambulance because you've grazed your knee.

Riding in a group is safer (ambitious overtaking manoeuvres excepted) and often more fun, but don't leave slower riders too far behind and give them a minute for a breather when they've caught up. Allow extra time for a group ride, as you'll inevitably stop and chat. You might need an extra top if you're standing around for a while. Ride within your ability, make sure you can slow down fast and give way to other users. Bells might be annoying, but they work. If you can't bring yourself to bolt one on, a polite 'excuse me' should be fine. **On hot, sunny days, slap on some Factor 30+ and** ALWAYS WEAR YOUR HELMET!

In the Event of an Accident

In the event of an accident requiring immediate assistance: Dial 999 and ask for POLICE or AMBULANCE. If you can supply the services with a grid reference of exactly where you are it should help to speed up their response time.

Rules of the (Off) Road

1. Always ride on legal trails.
2. Ride considerately – give way to horses and pedestrians.
3. Don't spook animals.
4. Ride in control – you don't know who's around the next corner.
5. Leave gates as you find them – if you're unsure, shut them.
6. Keep the noise down and don't swear loudly when you fall off in front of walkers.
7. Leave no trace – take home everything you took out.
8. Keep water sources clean – don't take toilet stops near streams.
9. Enjoy the countryside and respect its life and work.

Planning Your Ride

1. Consider the ability/experience of each rider in your group. Check the weather forecast. How much time do you have available? Now choose your route.
2. Study the route description before setting off, and cross-reference it with the relevant map.
3. Bear in mind everything we've suggested about safety, clothing, spares and food and drink.
4. Get out there and get dirty.

Maps & Symbols

Ordnance Survey maps are the most commonly used, are easy to read and many people are happy using them. If you're not familiar with OS maps and are unsure of what the symbols mean, you can download a free map legend from **www.ordnancesurvey.co.uk**

We've included details of the relevant OS map for each route. To find out more about OS maps or to order maps please visit **www.ordnancesurvey.co.uk**

Here's a guide to the symbols and abbreviations we use on the maps and in our directions:

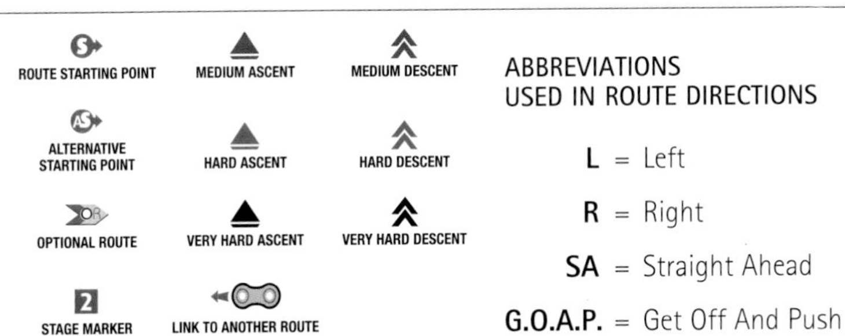

The Welsh Language (Cymraeg)

In a perfect world, we'd have produced this book in two languages but who wants to climb a mountain with a book that's twice as heavy and thick as it needs to be in their pocket? We have in the text, however, tried to explain meanings and pronunciations of key Welsh words to help non-speakers get a little insight into the local lingo, which is one of the oldest languages in Europe. The glossary opposite will also assist with the understanding of many of the place names mentioned. We hope the non Welsh speakers find this helpful and interesting, and that it meets with the approval of those that do speak the language.

Yr Iaith Gymraeg

Mewn byd perffaith, bydden ni wedi cyfieithu'r llyfr hwn i'r ddwy iaith, ond pwy sydd eisiau dringo mynydd gyda llyfr yn ei poced sydd ddwy waith mor drwm a sydd angen? Wedi dweud hynny, rydyn ni wedi ceisio esbonio ystyron rhai o brif eiriau'r Gymraeg, a sut i'w ynganu, er mwyn rhoi agoriad llygad i'r iaith lleol, yr iaith Ewropeaidd hynaf sy'n dal i gael ei ddefnyddio. Bydd y rhestr isod yn eich helpu i ddeall ystyr rhai o enwau'r lleoedd rydyn ni'n eu crybwyll. Rydyn ni'n gobeithio bydd y rhestr hon yn ddefnyddiol ac yn ddiddorol, ac yn dderbyniol i'r rhai hynny sydd yn siarad yr iaith Gymraeg.

ER COF AM
"WAYFARER"
1877 – 1956
UN OEDD YN CARU CYMRU
A LOVER OF WALES
ERECTED BY THE R.S.F.

A MONUMENT TO WM ROBINSON – THE WAYFARER – A TRUE PIONEER OF OFF-ROAD CYCLING (ROUTE 17)

Aber	Confluence or mouth of a river
Afon	River
Bach (also **Fach**)	Small
Betws	House of prayer
Blaen	Head of a valley
Bont (also **Pont**)	Bridge
Bryn	Hill
Bwlch	Pass or gap
Capel	Chapel
Carn	Pile of stones
Carreg	Stone
Castell	Castle
Cefn	Ridge
Coch	Red
Coed	Wood
Craig	Crag
Cwm	Valley or cirque
Dan (also **Tan**)	Below
Dwr	Water
Eglwys	Church
Esgair	Ridge
Fawr (also **Mawr**)	Big
Foel (also **Moel**)	Bare hill
Ffridd	Pasture
Ffordd	Road
Ffynnon	Well or spring
Glan	Bank or shore
Glyn	Valley
Hafod	Summer dwelling or pasture
Hen	Old
Isaf	Lower
Llan	A church, usually followed by the name of the saint to whom it's dedicated
Llwyn	A bush or grove
Llyn	Lake
Maes	Field
Mynydd (also **Fynydd**)	Mountain
Nant	Stream
Pant	Hollow
Pen	Top or end
Pentre	Village
Pwll	Pool
Rhiw	Slope
Rhos	Moorland
Rhyd	Ford
Tal	End or front
Tre (also **Tref**)	Homestead or town
Ty	House
Uchaf	Higher
Waun	Moorland or meadow
Ynys	Island
Ystrad	Wide valley

SECTION 1

South Wales
& the Brecon Beacons National Park

Lungbursting climbs over high mountains, stupendous drops from remote passes, sweeping singletrack above sumptuous beaches and the odd Roman road and ancient trade route thrown in for good measure. South Wales has something for everybody.

HIGH ABOVE THE TALYBONT RESERVOIR ON THE BRINORE TRAM ROAD (ROUTE 4)

RHOSSILI BAY (ROUTE 6)

South Wales & the Brecon Beacons National Park

route finder

SOUTH WALES AND THE BRECON BEACONS NATIONAL PARK

SINGLETRACK AND MINESHAFTS ON BAILEY'S TRAM ROAD

01 The Blorenge – Abergavenny Peaks 17km

Introduction

The lumbering limestone bulk of the Blorenge marks a watershed between the scenic Black Mountains and the pastoral Usk Valley, and the more 'lived in' landscapes of the once industrial South Wales 'valleys'. This route enjoys the best of both worlds, using tracks and trails left behind by the mining and quarrying to wind its way around the steep flanks of the mountain whilst enjoying wonderful views over Abergavenny and the Usk Valley to the towering peaks beyond. It's essentially a 'one up, one down' type of ride, although the up's a biggie, and the down's worth every turn of the pedals.

The Ride

There's something quite rewarding about a loop that starts easily and slowly turns up the wick as it goes. Travel-weary legs certainly won't be too shocked by the long, steady pull up the well-surfaced disused railway that forms a section of National Cycleway No. 46 and provides a great opportunity to spin before getting into the real meat of the route. But, even fully warmed up, they may baulk slightly as the gradient steepens on the lane that leads up onto Gilwern Hill. And it doesn't get any easier as the asphalt ends. Easy cruising follows – phew – a chance to get some glycogen back into those muscles before the big descent. It starts easy, with only a few boggy patches to skip around. But a stone-filled cutting sets the new benchmark, and the drop from the post will have most MTBers footing a few times as they balance over football-sized boulders with little choice of line. The rest is heavenly: sweeping singletrack that cuts a tasty diagonal across the mountain; and then easier broader stuff, mostly still with gravity on the right side. A final stiff pull gains the start of the last lane, and a lethal combo of leaves and rocks will punish those that don't carry enough speed.

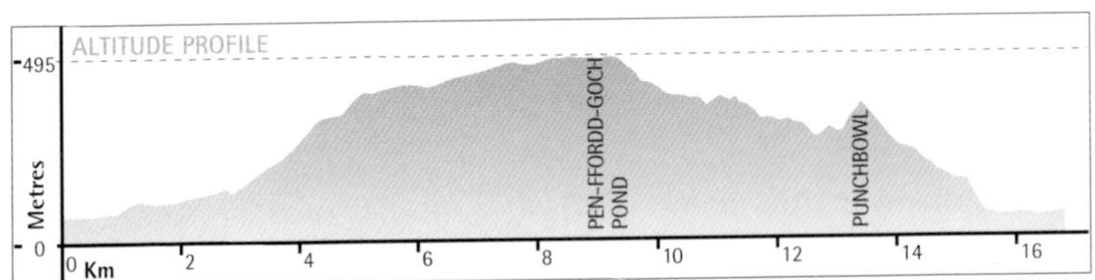

THE BLORENGE **GRADE: ▲**

TOTAL DISTANCE: 17KM » **TOTAL ASCENT**: 660M » **TIME**: 2-3 HOURS » **START/FINISH**: LLANFOIST CROSSING CAR PARK
START GRID REF: SO 286132 » **SATNAV**: LLANFOIST » **OS MAP**: EXPLORER OL13; LANDRANGER 161
PUB: LOTS OF CHOICE IN ABERGAVENNY » **CAFÉ**: LOTS OF CHOICE IN ABERGAVENNY

Directions – The Blorenge

S A well-surfaced track leads from the top of the car park (National Cycle Route 46). Follow this for over **4km**, crossing a road at one stage (Govilon Station), to another car park on the **R** (Forge Car Park).

2 Leave the trail through this car park and join the lane to continue in the same direction. Follow this **L** and then turn **L** to cross a bridge over the cycle path. Climb steeply up through a gate and past a farm and bear around to the **R** at the top. Continue for 300m and then bear sharp **L** onto a waymarked RUPP (Road Used as Public Path). Climb steeply past quarries and keep ahead to continue out onto a road at the very top. Turn **L** to ride past spoil heaps to the B4246.

3 Ride **SA** across the road into the Keeper's Pond Car Park and then turn sharp **L** to follow a well-surfaced track back on yourself and around the southern end of the pond and then along the western shore to it's northern tip. Cross the bridge and turn **R** to follow a clear track slightly uphill. This levels and then swings **R** to contour around the hillside, and then, shortly after a narrow cutting, bear **L** onto a narrow and steep singletrack, marked with a short post.

4 Drop to join a good track above woodland and keep **SA**, where it forks, to traverse on an old tram road. Pass a shaft to your **R**, and keep **SA** until you reach a gate that leads into the Devil's Punchbowl Nature Reserve.

5 Keep **SA** past the pond and climb steeply to a gate. Bear **L** to drop down a rough and stony track and then turn **R** onto the drive and then **L** onto the road to drop all the way back down into Llanfoist. Turn **L** onto the road at the bottom and then bear **L** at the T-junction to return to the car park.

Making a day of it

This is an isolated mountain so there's not a lot to go on. There are a few good trails on the other side of Abergavenny, in particular those that run around the western flanks of the Sugar Loaf (but none go to its summit). These could be used to link this ride to the **Black Mountains Classic** (page 11).

Making a weekend of it

The **Black Mountains Classic** (page 11), the **Mynydd Llangorse** (page 19) or **Gap Road** (page 25) are all within easy reach. The Cwmcarn trail centre isn't far away either.

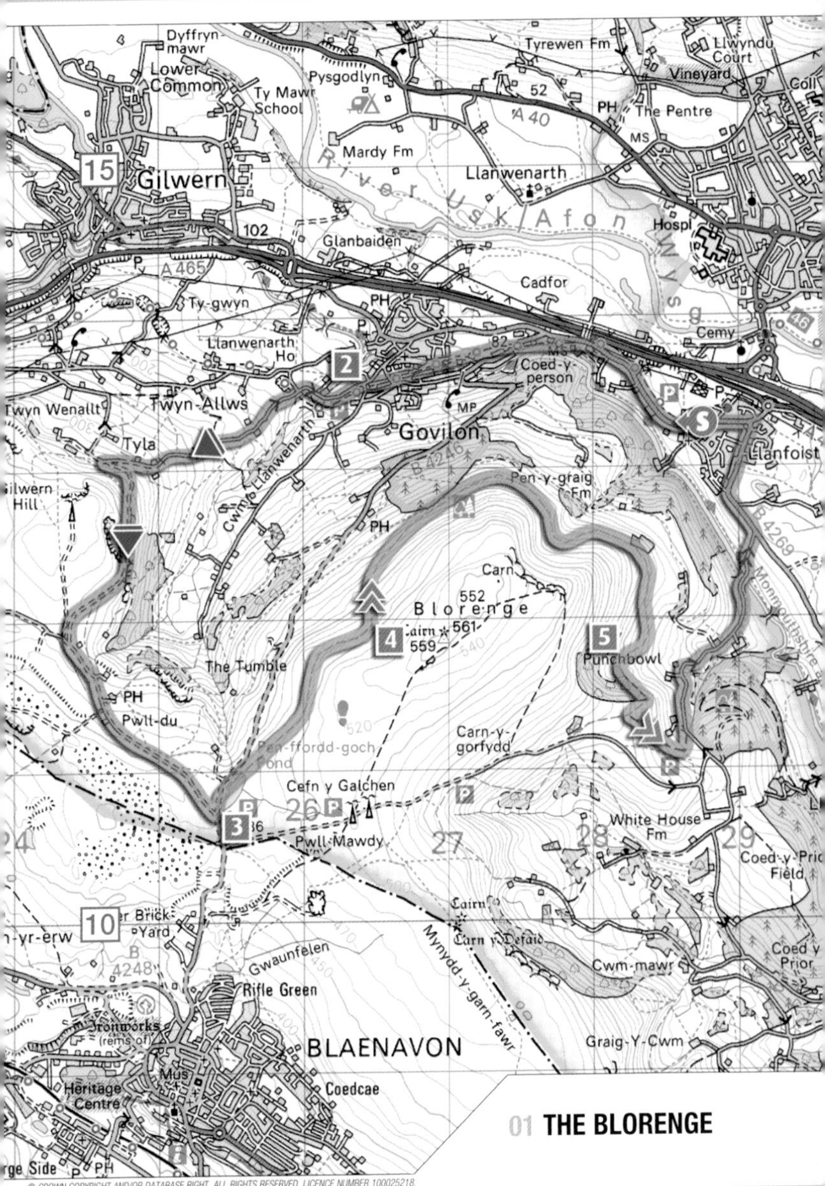

01 THE BLORENGE

ROUGH AND ROCKY ON RHIW TRUMAU

02 Black Mountains Classic

45.2km

Introduction

The valleys of the Grwyne Fawr and Grwyne Fechan slice deeply into the heart of the Black Mountains, nudging up against the highest peaks in the range, just a few kilometres north of the small town of Crickhowell. They are magnificent glens – broad and deep with spectacular rivers running through them – and they are both penetrated by some excellent trails that hurdle the lofty ridges that define them. These provide one of the longest, toughest and arguably best routes in this book.

The Ride

A good helping of steady road climbing gets the legs warmed up for the real action, and this starts abruptly at Tal-y-maes Bridge, where the full magnificence of the Grwyne Fechan first shows itself.

It's a long steady pull from there to the pass, and a 'clean' hinges on making it around the bend at the very top; it's painful to fail this close to the finish. Then it's full speed down Rhiw Trumau – don't get too carried away, it gets a bit stiff near the bottom. A little lane work leads over the next col – a break in the ridge of Y Grîb – and then it's the real killer, Y Dâs. It doesn't matter how good or fit you are, this is a carry, and it's a long and gruelling one too. It rewards though – the drop into the Grwyne Fawr Valley goes on forever. Just one up and one down left now. The up used to be horrible, but devious use of forest tracks provides a ride-able alternative to the obvious bridleway. And then it's the descent from Crug Mawr – a mix of sandy singletrack and rough and rocky – does mountain biking get any better?

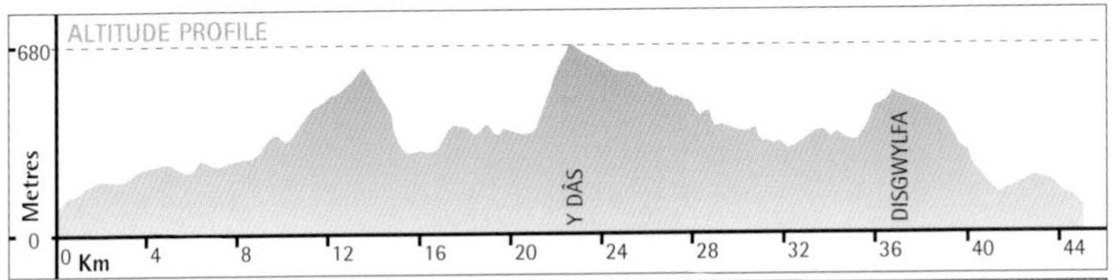

BLACK MOUNTAINS CLASSIC — **GRADE: ▲**

TOTAL DISTANCE: 45.2KM » **TOTAL ASCENT**: 1730M » **TIME**: 4–5 HOURS » **START/FINISH**: CRICKHOWELL
START GRID REF: SO 218183 » **SATNAV**: NP8 1BN » **OS MAP**: EXPLORER OL13; LANDRANGER 161
PUB: THE RED LION, LLANBEDR, TEL: 01873 810 754; PLENTY IN CRICKHOWELL » **CAFÉ**: PLENTY IN CRICKHOWELL

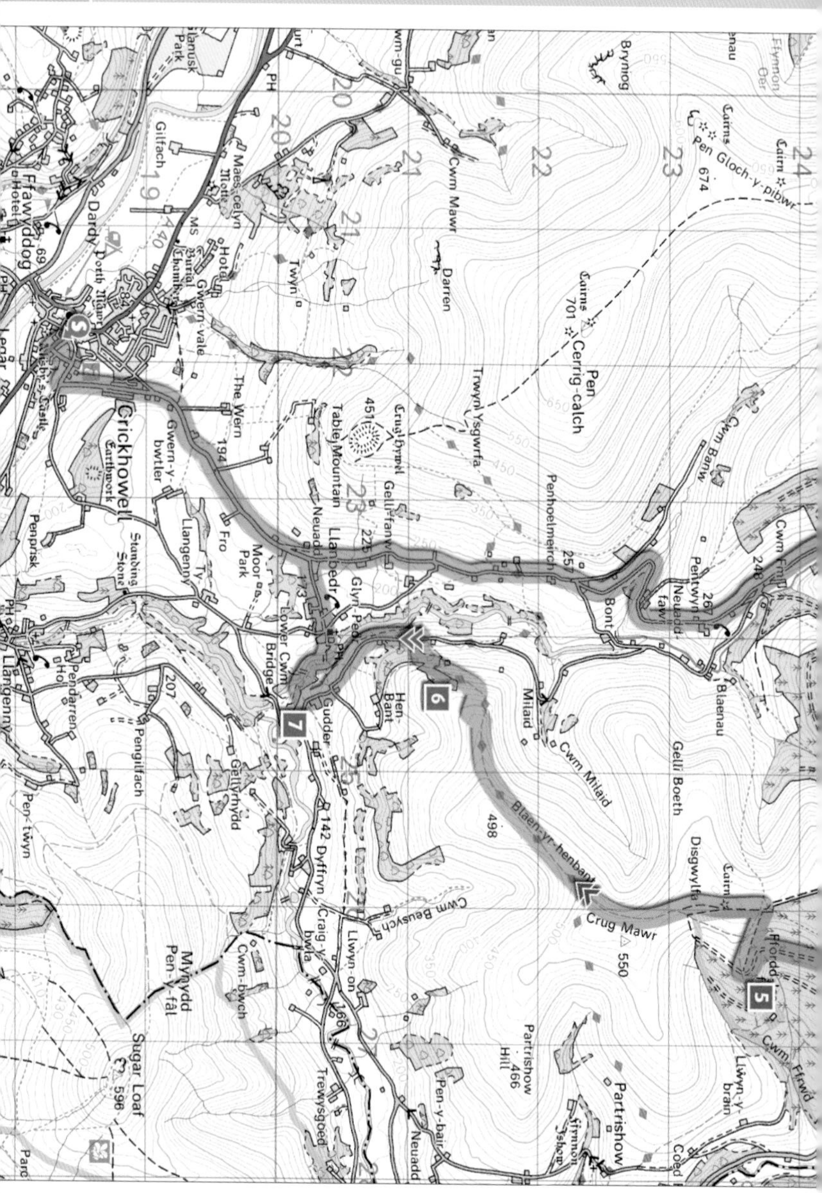

Crickhowell
Llanbedr
Table Mountain
Crug Hywel
Pen Cerrig-calch
Llangenny
Ffawyddog
Dardy
Gwernvale
Glangrwyney
Penhoelmeirch
Cwm Mawr
Darren
Twyn
Bryniog
Pen Gloch-y-pibwr
Cwm Banw
Pentwyn
Neuadd-fawr
Bont
Blaenau
Gelli Boeth
Milaid
Cwm Milaid
Blaen-yr-henbant
Crug Mawr
Disgwylfa
Ffordd-fawr
Cwm Ffrwd
Llwyn-y-brain
Partrishow
Partrishow Hill
Cwm Beusych
Llwyn-on
Pen-y-bair
Neuadd
Trewysgoed
Dyffryn Craig-y-bwla
Cwm-bwch
Mynydd Pen-y-fâl
Sugar Loaf
Gelltyrhydd
Pengilfach
Pen-twyn
Pendarren
Penprisk
Gudder
Lower Cwm Bridge
Glyn-Peg
Hen Bant
Moor Park
Gellifanw
Neuadd
The Wern
Gwern-y-bwtler
Fro
Standing Stone
Gilfach
Maes-celyn
Porth Mawr
Cwm-gu
Glanusk Park
Cairns
Earthwork
Motte

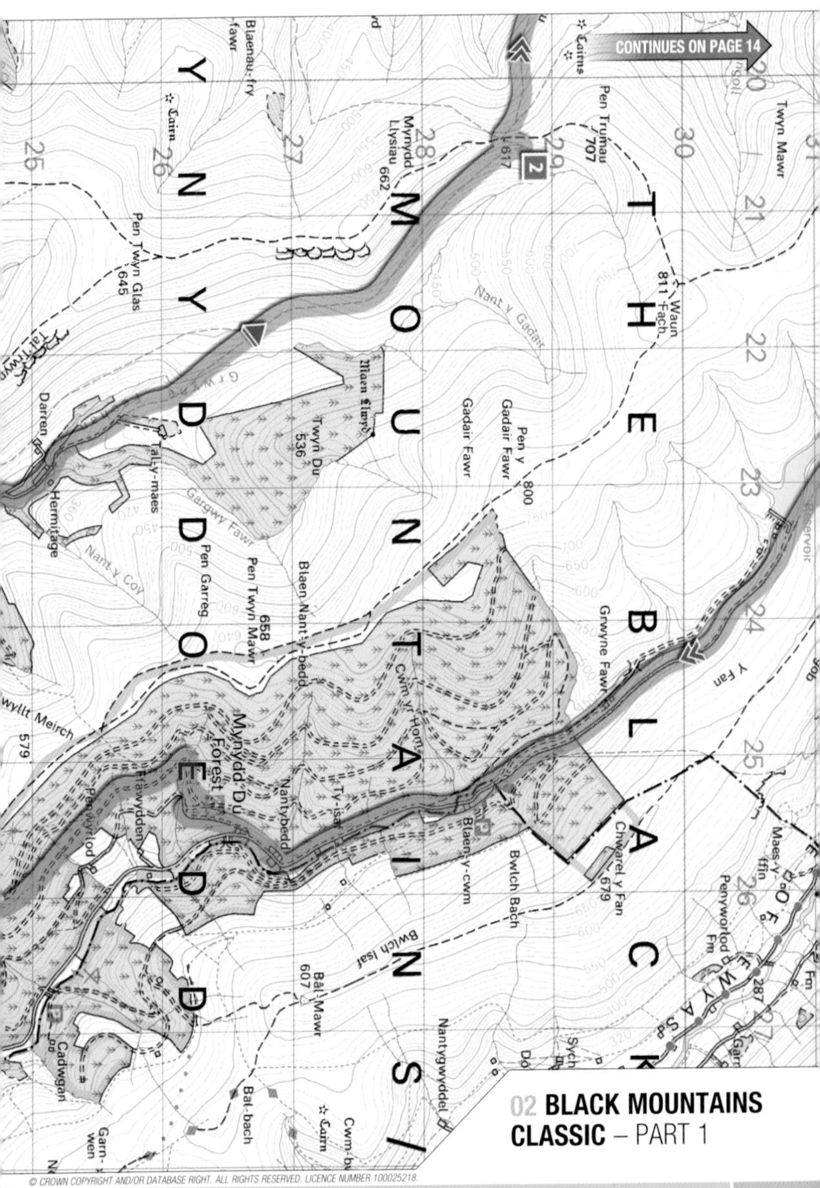

CONTINUES ON PAGE 14

02 BLACK MOUNTAINS CLASSIC – PART 1

02 BLACK MOUNTAINS CLASSIC – PART 2

CRUG MAWR SINGLETRACK PHOTO: JOHN COEFIELD

Directions – Black Mountains Classic

S Turn **L** out of the car park and **R** at the roundabout at the top of the road. Take the next **L** (signed *Grwynefechan*) and continue along this lane for 9km, keeping **SA** at a 3-way fork. At the road head, bear **L** up a stony climb. Bear **L** (effectively **SA**) through a gate and continue along a field edge to drop to Tal-y-maes Bridge. Cross the bridge and climb for another 3km to an obvious saddle.

2 Trend **R** and then **L** down the other side to pick up an obvious steep track that plummets down to a gate and eventually a road. Turn **R** onto this and continue **SA** to Grafog, where you turn **L** onto a steep track after a farm and climb up to the saddle between Castell Dinas and Y Grîb and down again to a junction at the edge of the open ground.

3 Turn **R** onto another track and follow this to the road at Blaenau Uchaf. Turn **R** and continue for 2km to a clear track on the **R**. Follow this onto open moorland and bear around to the **L** then **R** to climb the obvious stony trail straight up the steep hillside of Y Dâs (**G.O.A.P.**). At the top, keep **SA** on a sunken sandy trail.

4 Now descend across moorland past the Grwyne Fawr Reservoir to the road (**SA** at all gates). Continue down the road for 2km to a forest track on the **R**. Take this and keep **R** at the first fork and then **L** at the second, then **L** again to continue around the hillside until you reach a clearing with a rough track leading steeply up **R**. Follow this up to a junction with a forest track and turn **L** onto it. Follow this around the hillside for over 1km until it bends sharp **L** then sharp **R** then turn immediately **R** onto waymarked bridleway.

5 Take this up to a forest gate and keep **SA** on a singletrack that crosses open ground to t-into a traversing singletrack. Turn **L** onto this and follow it as it tracks below Crug Mawr summit and trig point, which is up to your left. Now continue around for 2.5km to a cairn where you turn **R**, off the main track, to drop steeply for 500m before veering **L** to traverse the hillside to a gate.

6 Don't go through the gate but turn sharp **R** for 10m and then **L** through another gate (marked *Permissive Bridleway*). Follow this down and around to the **R** and then, at a crossroads, take the second **L** to descend steeply to the road. Turn **L** and keep **SA** at the T-junction to continue for another 300m to a hedged track on the **R**.

7 Drop down to the riverbank and ride along it, passing one bridge and continuing to the second, which you cross. Climb steeply up the other side and keep **SA** in Llanbedr to pass the pub and continue out to a T-junction. Turn **L** to retrace your earlier tracks back to Crickhowell.

Making a weekend of it

The Blorenge (page 7), **Mynydd Llangorse** (page 19) and **The Gap Road** (page 25) are all within easy reach.

RED DUST SINGLETRACK ON MYNYDD LLANGORSE

03 Mynydd Llangorse – Black Mountains 31km

Introduction

Mynydd Llangorse is the westernmost peak of the Black Mountains, forming a lofty barrier between the Rhiangoll Valley and the River Usk. It's northern slopes mould into the southern flanks of the shapely outlier of Mynydd Troed, and its southernmost ridge dips steeply down to the village of Bwlch, which sits astride the A40. It's a fine peak, well-placed to offer great views back over the Rhiangoll to Waun Fach, the massif's highest ground; as well as to the mountains of the central Beacons on the far side of the River Usk. It also towers over the lake of the same name, which is the largest natural body of water in South Wales. This ride starts from its shores.

The Ride

The tracks and trails that run over and around Myndd Llangorse, and its subsidiary spurs of Cefn Moel and Pen Tir, are well worth exploring, especially in summer, when the red dusty earth allows the tyres to roll much more sweetly. But the only real way to make the most of them is to link them with some more agricultural going and a few country lanes, which make this quite a mixed outing. The highlights are without a doubt the sections that run across the mountain itself, particularly the singletrack along its western flanks and the descent from Cefn Moel to Bwlch. But the leg that crosses Allt yr Esgair is a welcome distraction too, especially as it takes you over a hilltop that sees far less exploration than most of the summits around here.

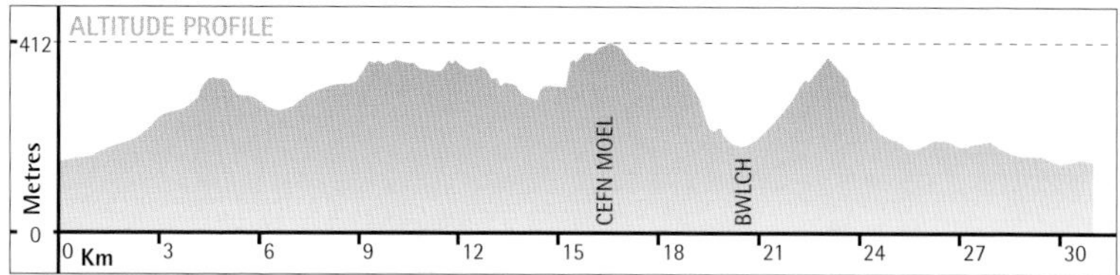

MYNYDD LLANGORSE **GRADE: ▲**

TOTAL DISTANCE: 31KM » **TOTAL ASCENT**: 820M » **TIME**: 3–4 HOURS » **START/FINISH**: LLANGORSE LAKE
START GRID REF: SO 128273 » **SATNAV**: LD3 7TR (NEAREST) » **OS MAP**: EXPLORER OL13; LANDRANGER 161
PUB: CASTLE INN, LLANGORSE, TEL: 01874 658 225 » **CAFÉ**: AT THE START

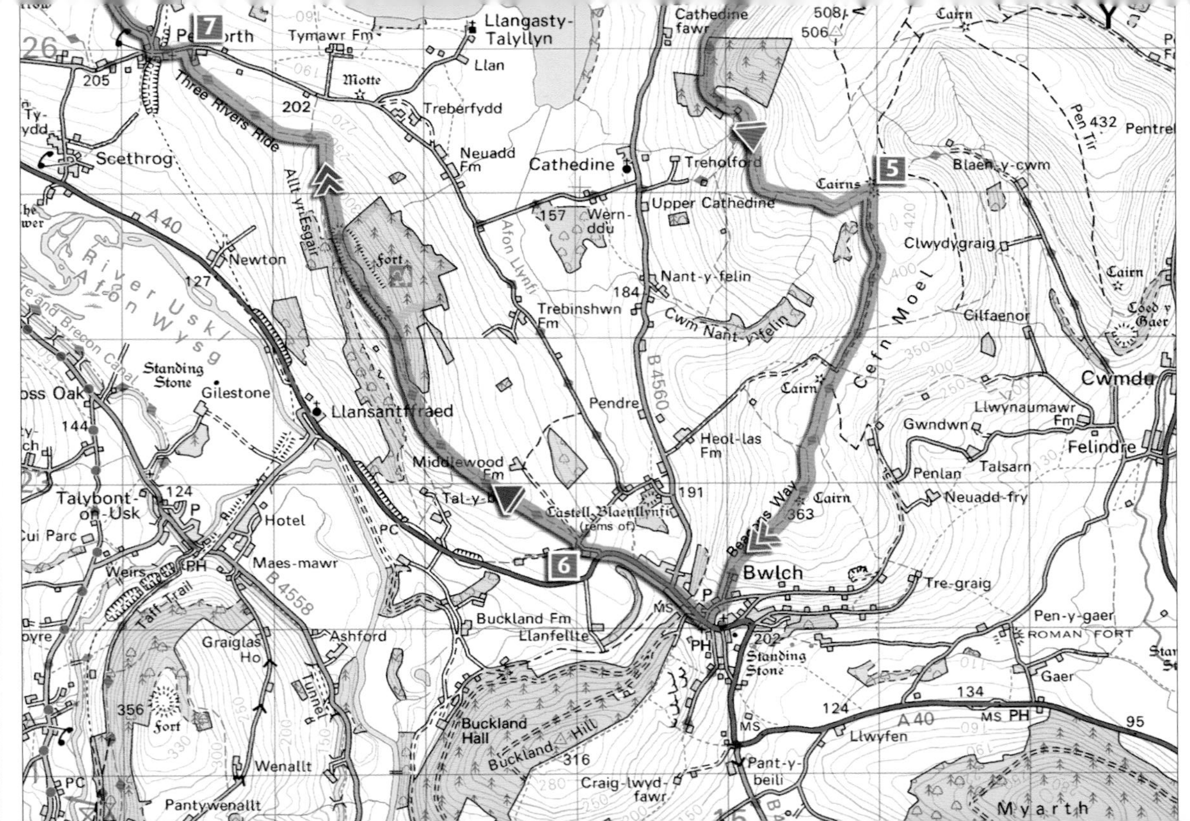
Scethrog
Talybont-on-Usk
Afon Wysg
River Usk
Brecon Canal
Standing Stone
Gilestone
Newton
Taff Trail
Graiglas Ho
Maes-mawr
Hotel
Tunnel
B4558
Ashford
Pantywenallt
Wenallt
Llansantffraed
Three Rivers Ride
Allt yr Esgair
Middlewood Fm
Buckland Hall
Buckland Hill
Buckland Fm
Llanfellte
Craig-lwyd-fawr
Llangasty-Talyllyn
Llan
Treberfydd
Tymawr Fm
Motte
Neuadd Fm
Cathedine
Afon Llynfi
Trebinshwn Fm
Pendre
Castell Blaenllynfi (rems of)
B4560
Upper Cathedine
Trehollford
Nant-y-felin
Cwm Nant-y-felin
Heol-las Fm
Bwlch
Beacons Way
Cairn
Cefn Moel
Cairns
Clwydygraig
Cilfaenor
Blaen-y-cwm
Gwndwn
Penlan
Llwynaumawr Fm
Talsarn
Neuadd-fry
Tre-graig
Felindre
Cwmdu
Pentre
Pen Tir
Pen-y-gaer
ROMAN FORT
Gaer
Llwyfen
A40
Pant-y-beili
Myarth
Cathedine fawr
fort

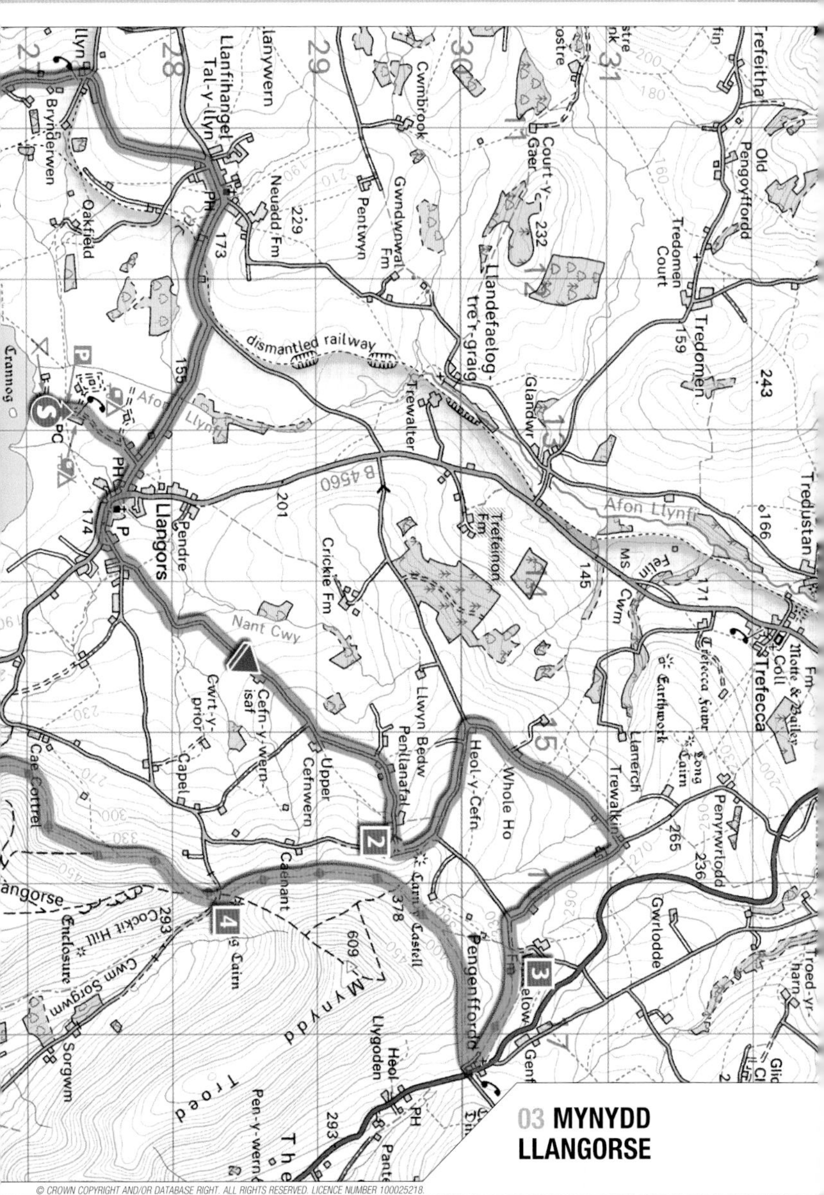

03 MYNYDD LLANGORSE

Directions – Mynydd Llangorse

S Ride back north out of the lake grounds and turn **R** then **R** again onto the B4560. Pass the Castle Inn on the left and then, after 100m, turn **L** (**NOT** the dead-end turning immediately after the pub). Fork **L** after 300m and climb for 3km to a T-junction.

2 Turn **L** and then, as the road bends right, keep **SA** on to a well-surfaced track. Drop to the road and turn **R**. Continue to a T-junction and turn **R** then, after 1km, turn **L** at another T-junction. Follow this past one bridleway on the right and then, as the road swings left, keep **SA**, through a gate, onto a bridleway that splits immediately. Take the **R** (higher) track.

3 Follow this around the hillside and through a gate onto a walled lane. Continue to another gate into a farmyard and turn **R**, onto a grassy bank that climbs between trees. Follow this out onto open ground and keep **SA**, ignoring an old quarry to the left. There are many trails here but keep **SA**, traversing the hillside, with the wall or fence down to your right. As long as you don't climb too high, or drop off of the open ground, you can't go wrong. All tracks arrive at a gate by a small road.

4 Keep **SA** and follow the **R** (lower) of 2 tracks that contour around the hill. Stay with this, keeping the open hillside to your left and fields to your right. Eventually you'll reach a wood, where you climb steeply, and then emerge onto a short section of singletrack across a meadow. Go through another gate and climb steeply for 500m to a corner. Continue straight up to a cairn at a crossroads.

5 Turn **R** and follow the main track for 4km down to Bwlch. Keep the wall to your right and don't be tempted to bear left at all. Drop to the road and turn **R** towards the A40. Turn **R** onto this and continue for 1km to a turning on the **R** (Beacon Farm Shop).

6 Turn **R** here and then turn **immediately L** onto a bridleway. Climb up to a gate that leads onto open ground and keep **SA** and slightly **L** to another gate. Continue over the crest of the hill and keep **SA** to drop through the bracken and trees to the road.

7 Turn **L** and then **R** at the T-junction. Continue to another junction and keep **SA**. Turn **R** into Llanfihangel Tal-y-llyn and follow the signs back to Llangorse. Turn **R** back to the lake.

Making a day of it

The main crossing of Mynydd Llangorse could easily be linked into the **Black Mountains Classic** (page 11) although it would make a very big ride even bigger.

Making a weekend of it

There are stacks of great natural trails around here so there really should be no shortage of alternatives. Most local are **The Blorenge** (page 7), the **Black Mountains Classic** (page 11), and of course, **The Gap Road** (page 25), which kicks off in neighbouring Talybont-on-Usk.

DESCENDING CEFN MOEL INTO BWLCH

RED RUBBLE ON THE BRINORE TRAM ROAD

04 The Gap Road – Brecon Beacons 34km

Introduction

The Brecon Beacons are not just the highest peaks in South Wales, they are the tallest in all of Southern Britain, and their distinctive table-topped summits are recognisable from miles around. There are no trails over the tallest peaks – Pen y Fan and Corn Du – but the ridge that they crown is crossed by an ancient road that hurdles an atmospheric pass between two equally impressive mountains just a couple of kilometres to the east. The pass is named is Bwlch ar y Fan, which means 'Gap in the peaks.' It's more commonly referred to as simply 'The Gap' and has earned almost legendary status with Beacons MTBers.

The Ride

Despite its length and the amount of ascent involved, this is effectively a two up, two down expedition. The clamber up onto the Brinore Tram Road starts easily enough, but it ups the ante near the top and anyone pulling up onto the ridge without stopping can consider themselves very capable. The road itself is mainly well-surfaced and only slightly undulating, but the views from it are gobsmacking. And then it's a fast and frantic drop to the valley floor to head north to the main attraction.

The Gap is totally rideable. Sadly the climb out of the ravine at the very bottom of the trail isn't, so any attempt to clean the whole thing needs to start after this. Once out of the ravine, the climb is straightforward, so energy can be conserved for the descent. This starts immediately after the gate, and steepens straight away. The final few steps are the worst, and then it's a sweeping left-hand bend – still tricky – a couple of easier steps, and then a wonderful 3km down the side of the valley. Don't forget to take five and look back; the headwall of Cwm Cynwyn is a fine natural amphitheatre.

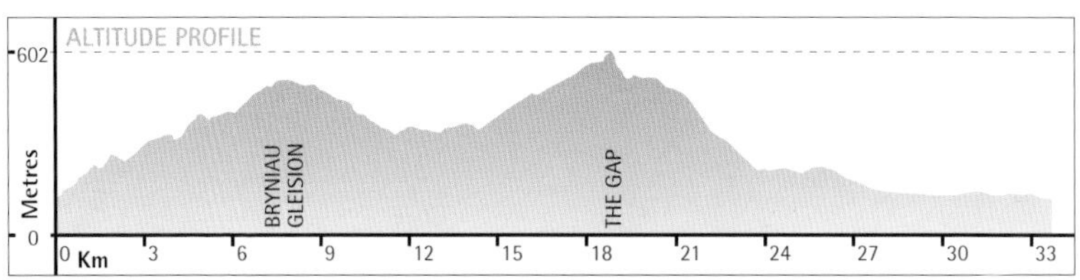

THE GAP ROAD – BRECON BEACONS **GRADE: ▲**

TOTAL DISTANCE: 34KM » **TOTAL ASCENT**: 950M » **TIME**: 4-5 HOURS » **START/FINISH**: TALYBONT-ON-USK
START GRID REF: SO 115225 » **SATNAV**: TALYBONT-ON-USK » **OS MAP**: EXPLORER OL12; LANDRANGER 160 & 161
PUB: LOTS OF CHOICE IN TALYBONT-ON-USK » **CAFÉ**: TALYBONT STORES, CAFE AND POST OFFICE, TALYBONT-ON-USK

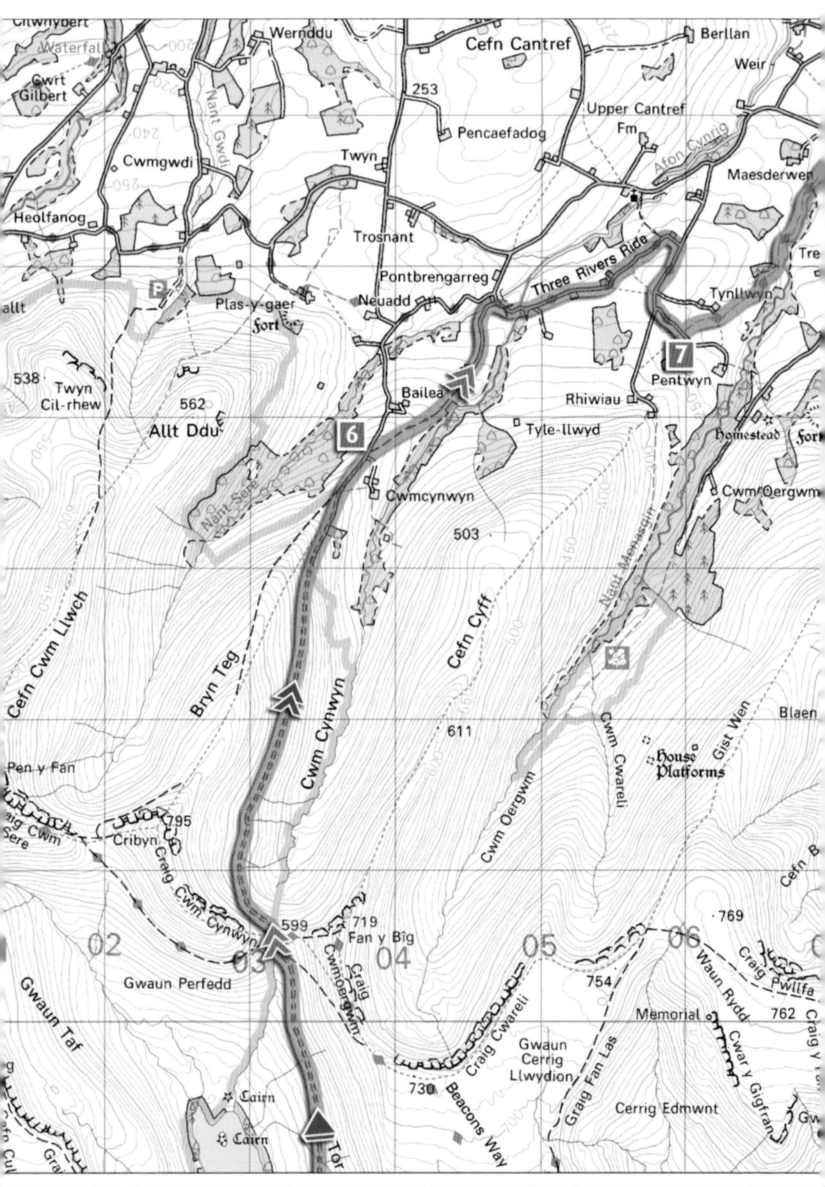
Cefn Cantref
Berllan
Weir
Wernddu
Waterfall
Cwrt Gilbert
253
Upper Cantref Fm
Pencaefadog
Nant Gwdi
Cwmgwdi
Twyn
Afon Cynrig
Maesderwen
Heolfanog
Trosnant
Three Rivers Ride
Pontbrengarreg
Tynllwyn
Plas-y-gaer
Fort
Neuadd
7
538
Twyn Cil-rhew
562
Bailea
Pentwyn
Rhiwiau
Allt Ddu
6
Tyle-llwyd
Homestead
Cwmcynwyn
Cwm Oergwm
Nant Sere
503
Nant Menasgin
Cefn Cyff
Cefn Cwm Llwch
Bryn Teg
Cwm Cynwyn
611
Blaen
Cwm Cwareli
House Platforms
Gist Wen
Pen y Fan
795
Cribyn
Craig Cwm Sere
Craig Cwm Cynwyn
Cwm Oergwm
599
719
Fan y Bîg
769
02
03
04
05
06
Gwaun Perfedd
754
Craig Pwllfa
Gwaun Taf
Craig Cwmoergwm
Waun Rydd
Memorial
762
Craig Cwareli
Gwaun Cerrig Llwydion
Graig Fan Las
Cwar y Gigfran
Cairn
730
Beacons Way
Cerrig Edmwnt
Tor

CONTINUES ON PAGE 29

04 THE GAP ROAD – BRECON BEACONS – PART 1

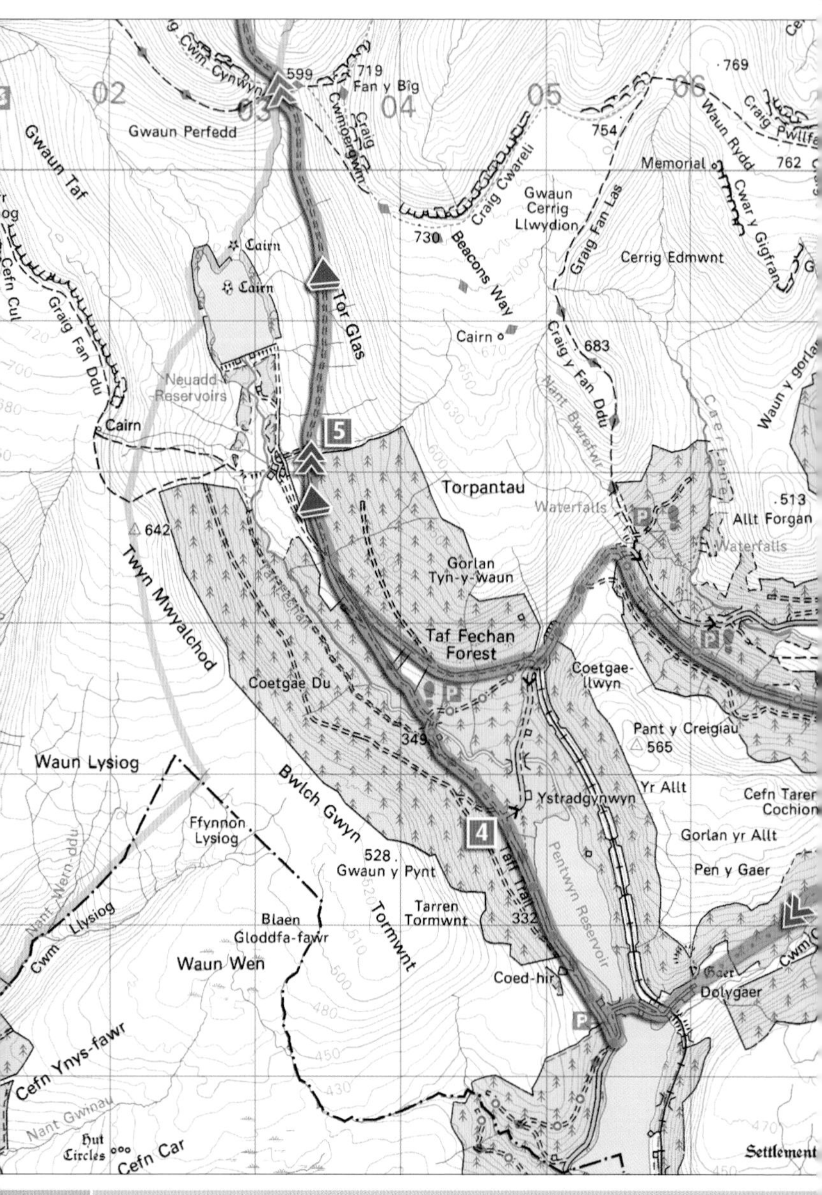

Fan y Bîg
719
599
Gwaun Perfedd
Gwaun Taf
Craig Cwareli
Gwaun Cerrig Llwydion
Craig Fan Las
Cerrig Edmwnt
Beacons Way
Tor Glas
Neuadd Reservoirs
Cairn
Craig Fan Ddu
Craig y Fan Ddu
Torpantau
Waterfalls
Allt Forgan
Gorlan Tyn-y-waun
Taf Fechan Forest
Twyn Mwyalchod
Coetgae Du
Coetgae-llwyn
Pant y Creigiau
565
Waun Lysiog
Bwlch Gwyn
Ystradgynwyn
Yr Allt
Cefn Tarren Cochion
Gorlan yr Allt
Pen y Gaer
Ffynnon Lysiog
Gwaun y Pynt
528
Tarren Tormwnt
Tormwnt
Blaen Gloddfa-fawr
Waun Wen
Coed-hir
Pentwyn Reservoir
Dolygaer
Cefn Ynys-fawr
Cefn Car
Hut Circles
Settlement
Taff Trail
Memorial
Waun Rydd
Cwar y Gigfran
Craig Pwllfa
769
754
762
730
683
642
513
349
332

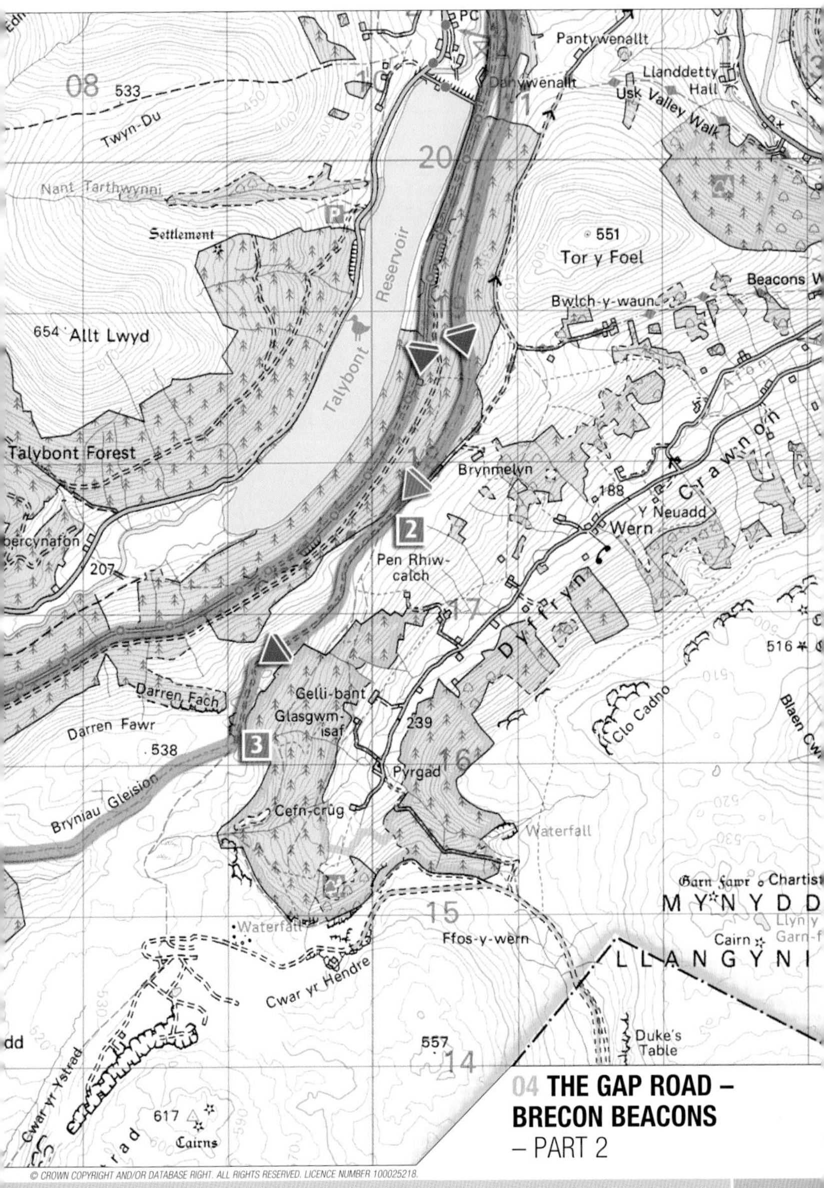

04 THE GAP ROAD – BRECON BEACONS – PART 2

Directions – The Gap Road – Brecon Beacons

S Turn off of the main street onto the waymarked Taff Trail (next to the White Hart) and climb the steep concrete ramp that leads over the canal. Follow this over a bridge and then stay on the main track as it climbs steadily around the hillside. Go **SA** at a crossroads after 1.8km (signed *Bryn Ore Tramroad Trefil*) and then fork **L** at another junction. Go **SA** at another forest road, all the time staying on the waymarked Brinore Tramroad. A short steep climb leads to a junction with the road on the top of the ridge.

Optional Route – Short cut

OR Start on the Taff Trail as above but stay on the Taff Trail for 10km to join the road at Torpantau. Turn **L** and descend over a cattle grid to a broad forest track on the right. Turn **R** here and keep **R** at the immediate fork. Continue around the hillside, ignoring a forest track on the right, and drop to the road at a four-way junction (see point 4). Turn **R** onto another track (signed *No Vehicles Except 1-31 March, 1-15 Sept*) and follow the main route from there (near the end of point 4).

2 Turn **R** (signed *Dolygaer*) and follow this broad track for 1.5km to a gate in a narrow pass at Pen Bwlch Glascwm. Keep ahead to climb steeply to the top and here bear **R**, off the main track, onto a rutted track.

3 Follow this across moorland to the edge of the forest and drop steeply down, keeping **SA** at a new forest road, to join the road at the bottom, by the Outdoor Centre. Keep **SA** to cross the dam and then turn **R**. Continue to a turning on the **L** (signed *Talybont-on-Usk 8.5*).

4 Turn **L** here and follow it up past another turning on the right, before crossing a bridge by some waterfalls. Continue past a large car park on the left to a junction with two tracks on the right, on a left-hand bend (short cut joins here). Turn **R** on to the second of these tracks (signed *No Vehicles Except 1-31 March, 1-15 Sept*) and climb then drop into a ravine.

5 Climb out of this and continue upwards to the obvious pass in the mountains – The Gap. Ride straight through this and drop for around 3km to a gate. Keep **SA** to the road head.

6 There are three gates on the right and one on the left. Take the middle (wooden) one on the **R**, and follow the narrow, rocky drop all the way to a T-junction, where you turn **R**. Stay on this for 1.5km to another T-junction and turn **R** again. Fork **L** after 500m and then, 300m further on, turn **L** onto a bridleway (legally diverted footpath).

7 Follow the left-hand edge of the field down to the stream and continue to follow bridleway waymarks, with the Nant Menasgin down to your right, to the road. Turn **R** and then **R** again into Llanfrynach. Turn **R** in the village, by a telephone box, to follow the road (Taff Trail) to Pencelli. Here continue on the road, following signs to Talybont-on-Usk.

Making a day of it

It's long enough already but it is possible to swing left rather than right after dropping down from the Gap, and follow narrow lanes and the old road around to the Storey Arms on the A470. This can be linked with the Taff Trail a bit further south and can be followed into Garwnant Forest, where other forest tracks lead down to the outskirts of Merthyr Tydfil. Pick up the Taff Trail here and follow it up into the mountains again.

Making a half day of it

Using the Taff Trail to eliminate the climb onto the Brinore Tramroad, it's possible to make a shorter (31km) loop with less climbing. See the **Optional Route** opposite.

ON THE BRINORE TRAM ROAD, HIGH ABOVE THE TALYBONT RESERVOIR

SARN HELEN – WHAT THE ROMANS DID FOR US!

05 Sarn Helen & Fforest Fawr 21km

Introduction

The Romans didn't have an easy time in Wales; fierce resistance from the locals prevented them from gaining any real foothold in the principality. But they did manage to build one seriously good trail – Sarn Helen – which runs from Carmarthen, right down in the south-west, to Caernarfon, on the north coast. Winding by their standards, it straddles high mountains and bleak moors and is peppered with enough history and folk law to have warranted several books dedicated purely to it. It also inspired a classic Welsh language track by the Super Furry Animals – "Down in the valley, there's a road for you and me". This ride focuses on a stretch of the road that crosses the Fforest Fawr mountain range, in the heart of the Brecon Beacons National Park.

The Ride

This is one of the easiest loops in the book. And the navigation's easy too, so it's a great one for those looking to gain a bit of Beacons experience before stretching themselves a bit more. The crux is the section of Sarn Helen that leads from Coed y Rhaiadr up to the Afon Llia – nearly 8km in total. It's a mix of fairly well-surfaced double track with the odd patch of slick rock, and a few sections of steeper, rocky stuff that tests the mettle a little more. The crossing of the Afon Nedd Fechan used to be exciting, fording a deep and often fast-flowing river. But this worry has been removed now with the installation of a shiny new FSC footbridge. The bridge doesn't make the climb up the other side any easier though, but it's the last one of any note anyway so enjoy the workout. The final leg, across the limestone pavement splattered Carnau Gwynion wraps it all up nicely.

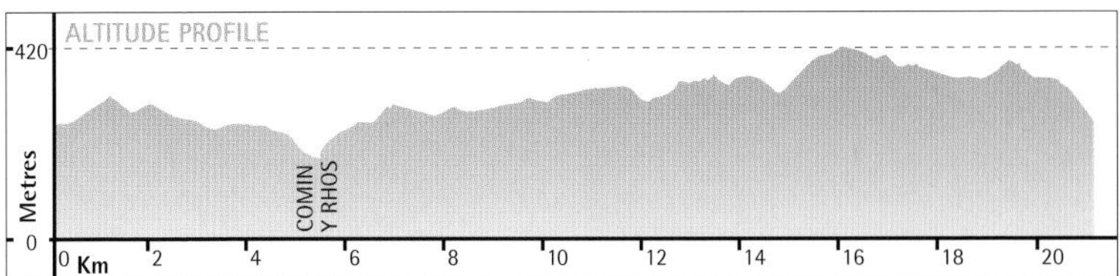

SARN HELEN & FFOREST FAWR **GRADE: ▲**

TOTAL DISTANCE: 21KM » **TOTAL ASCENT**: 570M » **TIME**: 2-3 HOURS » **START/FINISH**: YSTRADFELLTE CAR PARK
START GRID REF: SN 929134 » **SATNAV**: CF44 9JE » **OS MAP**: EXPLORER OL12; LANDRANGER 160
PUB: THE NEW INN, YSTRADFELLTE, TEL: 01639 720 211 » **CAFÉ**: WATERFALLS CAFE IN THE VILLAGE HALL, YSTRADFELLTE

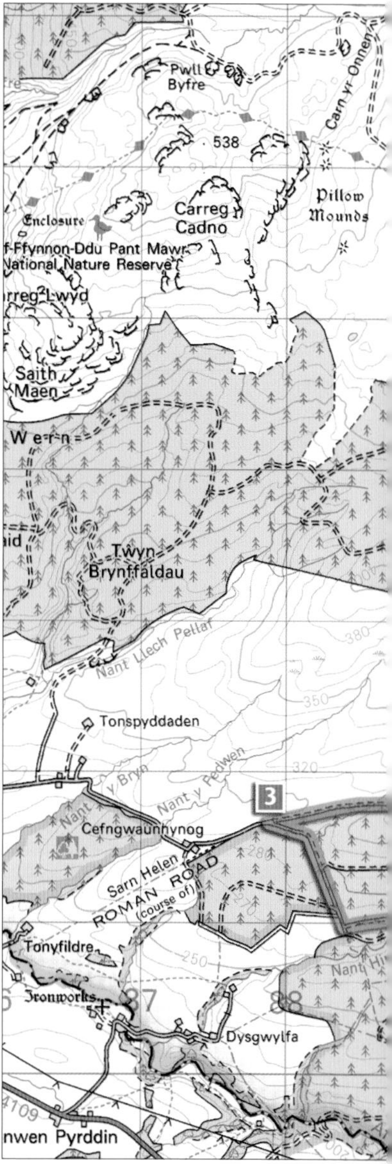
Pwll Byfre
538
Carn yr Onnen
Carreg Cadno
Pillow Mounds
Enclosure
f-Ffynnon-Ddu Pant Mawr National Nature Reserve
rreg Lwyd
Saith Maen
W e r n
Twyn Brynffaldau
Nant Llech Pellaf
380
350
Tonspyddaden
320
Nant y Bryn
Nant y Fedwen
3
Cefngwaunhynog
Sarn Helen
ROMAN ROAD (course of)
Tonyfildre
250
Ironworks
Dysgwylfa
87
88
4109
nwen Pyrddin

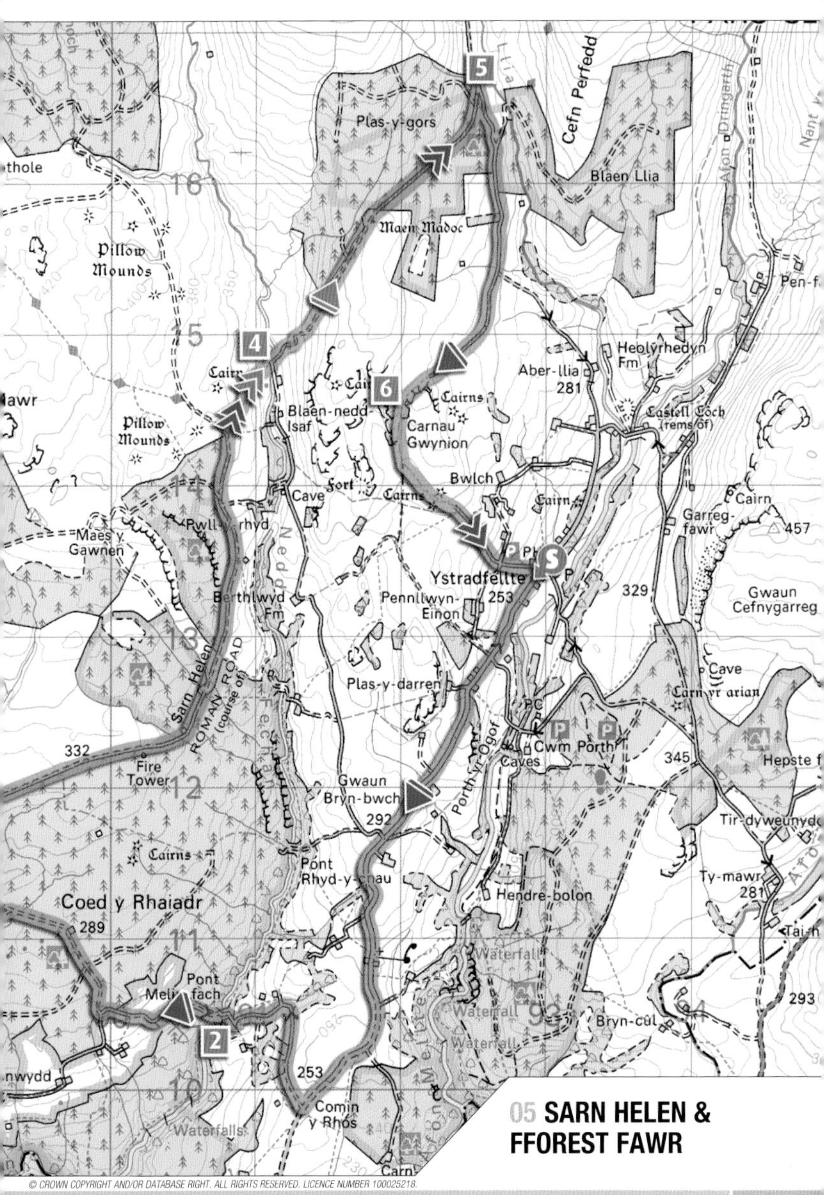
05 SARN HELEN & FFOREST FAWR
Plas-y-gors
Cefn Perfedd
Blaen Llia
Maen Madoc
Pillow Mounds
Heolyrhedyn Fm
Aber-llia
281
Castell Coch (rems of)
Cairns
Blaen-nedd-Isaf
Carnau Gwynion
Bwlch
Cave
Fort
Cairn
Garreg-fawr
457
Maes y Gawnen
Pwll-y-rhyd
Ystradfellte
253
Pennllwyn-Einon
329
Gwaun Cefnygarreg
Berthlwyd Fm
Sarn Helen
ROMAN ROAD (course of)
Plas-y-darren
Carn yr arian
Cwm Porth
Caves
Porth yr Ogof
345
Hepste
332
Fire Tower
Gwaun Bryn-bwch
292
Tir-dyweunydd
Cairns
Pont Rhyd-y-cnau
Ty-mawr
281
Coed y Rhaiadr
289
Hendre-bolon
Waterfall
Pont Melin-fach
Bryn-cul
293
253
Comin y Rhos
Waterfalls
Carn

Directions – Sarn Helen & Fforest Fawr

S Turn **R** out of the car park and follow the road for 4km to a junction with a small lane to the right (signed *Pont Melin-fach*). Turn **R** and drop to the bridge and picnic area, and then climb steeply back up towards the forest.

2 Turn **R** over the cattle-grid onto a good forest track and stay on this 1km, where you turn **L** onto another broad, well-surfaced track. Follow this to a T-junction and turn **R**, then keep **SA** at a left fork to climb easily. At the next T-junction, turn **R**, and then keep **SA** at a fork to another junction where you keep **SA** again to a tarmac lane.

3 Turn **sharp R** onto Sarn Helen and follow this as it climbs and dips often; following the edge of the forest at first, and then veering northwards above the Afon Nedd Fechan. Stay on the main track, which is well waymarked, until it eventually leaves the forest and drops down to the Afon Nedd Fechan, where there's a new footbridge.

4 Cross the bridge and climb steeply on a rubble track towards Plas-y-gors Forest (you'll pass a large standing stone called Maen Madoc on your right). Keep **SA** into the forest and descend to the road, where you turn **R**.

5 Drop for nearly 1km to a sharp left-hand turn with a walled track on the right; take this track (effectively **SA**). Climb steadily towards Carnau Gwynion and after 1km you'll come to a gate near the top: go through this and follow a faint grassy track that trends **L**, keeping the crags to your left.

6 This leads between the two summits, past an old lime kiln, and then descends to gate. Go through the gate and continue downhill on a broad track. This drops back into Ystradfellte, where you'll pass the car park.

Making a day of it

The Roman road carries on both south and north, and both have their interesting moments, especially northwards around the flanks of Fan Frynach. This could be ridden from the road at the Afon Llia as far as Forest Lodge, and then quiet, but brutally steep, lanes could be used to get back on the route again.

Making a weekend of it

The Gap Road (page 25) is the nearest to here, and there are a couple of variations to try there, depending on how strong you are feeling. This is also the nearest outing to Afan Argoed if you fancy some trail centre action.

SANDY SINGLETRACK ABOVE THE BEACH AT RHOSSILI

06 Rhossili and The Gower

35km

Introduction

The Gower Coast was Britain's first Area of Outstanding Natural Beauty and it's not difficult to see why, with some of the finest beaches and most spectacular sea cliff scenery in the UK. But it's not all golden sands and pounding surf; the spine of the slender peninsula consists of a lofty, whaleback ridge that's criss-crossed with tracks and trails just made for MTBing. It's not a big area, the whole peninsula measures less than 20km from start to tip, and it's barely 12km across at its widest point, so there isn't loads of choice. But what there is definitely makes it worth the trip west.

The Ride

It's all about one trail really – a narrow ribbon of sandy singletrack slung between the villages of Langennith and Rhossili. For just a few kilometres, you could have been transported to anywhere in the world, with incredible views over one of the finest beaches you'll ever see anywhere. But don't take your eyes off the rollercoaster trail for too long, this one needs concentration. But that's not to say the rest of the route's not worth the effort though; it is. The climb onto Cefn Bryn at the start gets tougher the higher you go, and the run along the ridge top is pure fun – even better as you get to ride it both ways. Then there's a gnarly drop to the packhorse bridge over Burry Pill and the equally steep climb out of it. Throw in a couple of exceptional pubs along the way and this one'll definitely have you grinning from ear to ear.

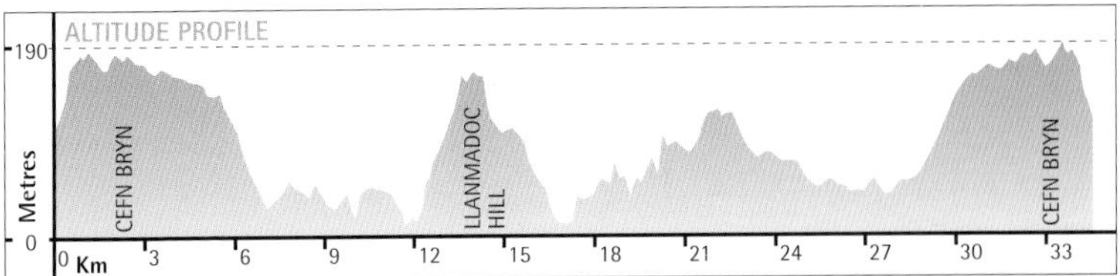

RHOSSILI AND THE GOWER **GRADE: ▲**

TOTAL DISTANCE: 35KM » **TOTAL ASCENT**: 750M » **TIME**: 3.5–4.5 HOURS » **START/FINISH**: PENMAEN
START GRID REF: SS 528887 » **SATNAV**: PENMAEN » **OS MAP**: EXPLORER 164; LANDRANGER 159
PUB: THE KING ARTHUR, REYNOLDSTON, TEL: 01792 390 775 » **CAFÉ**: THE BAY BISTRO, RHOSSILI, TEL: 01792 390 519; THE KING'S HEAD, LLANGENNITH, TEL: 01792 386 212

Hills Tor
Prissen's Tor
Hills
Cwm Ivy
Marsh
North Hill Tor
Tor-gro
North Hill Fm
Broughton Bay
Foxhole Pt
Twlc Pt
Dunes
Llanmadoc
Phillestone Fm
Cheriton
Bovehill Castle
Kittlehill
Broughton Burrows
Delvid
Cairns
The Bulwark
Penmynydd
Burry Pill
Llanmadoc Hill
Ryer's Down
Cockstreet
Tankeylake Moor
Llangennith Moors
Kennexstone
Llangennith
Burry Green
Coety Green
Hardingsdown
Hillend
Hillend Burrows
Forts
Hardings Down
Burnt Mound
Rhossili Down
Druids Lodge
White Moor
Cathan
East Cathan
Druids Moor
Earthwork
Burry
Standing Stones
Sweyne's Howes
Burial Chambers
Burnt Mounds
Sluxton
Betlands
Henllys
Lake Fm
Standing Stone
Kingshall
Llanddewi
Castle
Cairns
The Beacon
Earthwork
Church (rems of)
Rhossili
Talgarth's Well
Scurlage
Middleton
Pitton
Pitton Cross
Kimleymoor
Monksland
Fort
Fall Bay
Pilton
Pilton Green
Tears Point
Mewslade Bay
Thurba
Cave
Red Chamber
Margam
Moor Corner Fm
Gower Coast National Nature Reserve
Paviland Manor
The Knave
Littlehills

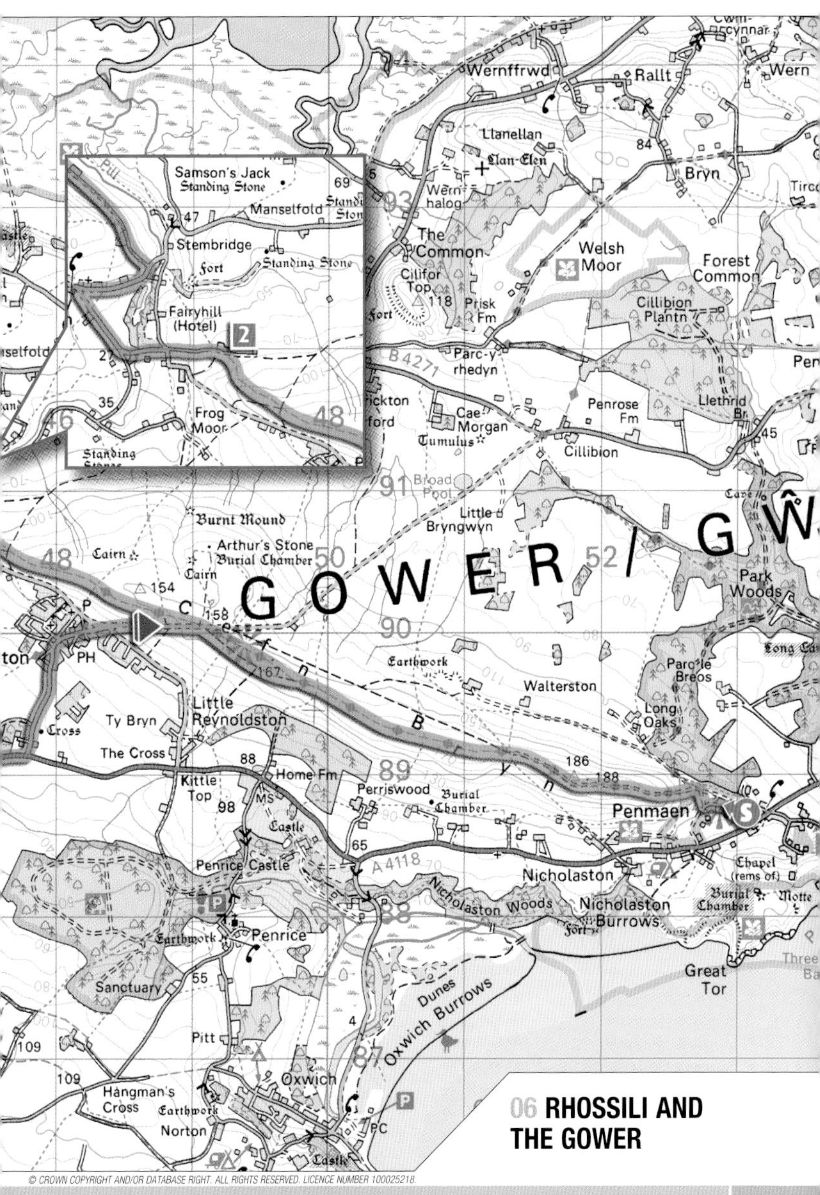

06 RHOSSILI AND THE GOWER

Directions – Rhossili and the Gower

S Turn **L** out of the car park and immediately **R** onto a rough track. Climb to another track and bear **L**. Follow this along the ridge top for 4km to a road. Keep **SA**, to continue in exactly the same direction on a grassy track that leads to a trig point. Fork **L** here to continue along the crest of the ridge, and stay on the main track, avoiding any left forks, until you drop **R** to a drive above Hillend.

2 Bear **L** onto this and continue to a crossroads; go **SA**. Continue to a T-junction and turn **R** (towards Burry Green and Llangennith) and continue into Burry Green. Turn **R** at the green, and then, after 600m, bear **L** onto waymarked bridleway. Follow this past some houses and then down to cross a packhorse bridge. Climb steeply up the other side and follow the road around to the left at the top.

3 Turn **L** onto the road and follow it into Cheriton, where you turn **sharp L** by the Brittania Inn. Climb for 700m, **ignoring** one bridleway on the right, and then turn **R** onto a gravel track. Follow this up on to Llanmadoc Hill and stay with it until it ends by a cottage. Keep ahead until you reach open ground, and then turn **half L** to drop to a gravel drive. Turn **R** onto this to the road.

4 Turn **R** onto the road and keep **SA** in the village, with the pub to your right. Continue to a mini roundabout and turn **L** (towards Hillend). Follow the road down to the entrance to the caravan site and go **L** through a bridlegate. Turn immediately **R** (not up the hill) and follow the narrow track parallel to the wall. Stay with this all the way up to the road at Rhossili and turn **L** towards Middleton. Continue for 700m to a turning on the **L** by Jessamine Farm.

5 Turn **L** here and follow this up until it becomes a dirt track, and stay with it to the end where a gate gives access to a green lane that leads off to the **R**. Follow this through Kingshall Farm (derelict) and across a couple of fields to join another green lane. This leads to Lake Farm where it turns **L** to the road.

6 Turn **R** towards the A4118, and then turn **L** onto this. Follow this for 1.4km to a road on the **L** (Reynoldston). Climb through the village and up past the King Arthur Hotel. Continue **SA** ahead to the top, where you turn **R** to retrace your outward journey along Cefn Bryn and back to the car park.

Making a day of it

This route makes the most of the best trails in the area; some of the inland bridleways can get a bit agricultural. However, you could lengthen things with a crossing of the top of Hardings Down, or you could just spend a few hours on the beach.

Making a weekend of it

Keep heading west for the **Preseli Hills** loop (page 45). Or track back east to Afan Argoed. Or, again, just chill out on the beach!

SANDY SINGLETRACK WITH BURRY HOLMS IN THE DISTANCE

07 Preseli Hills – Pembrokeshire 37km

Introduction

Man first established a foothold in the Preseli Hills nearly 5,000 years ago. Later, they became a major trade route between England and Ireland and, as traffic increased, the hills became the setting for many stories and legends. King Arthur crossed the hills in pursuit of the legendary boar, Twrch Trwyth; and St Brynach sought sanctuary here before finally settling in the nearby village of Nevern. It's an amazingly atmospheric place with burial cairns and standing stones lining the paths, and rocky tors crowning the hills. It was from one of these, Carn Menyn, that the bluestones that now form the inner circle of Stonehenge were taken.

The Ride

Pembrokeshire may not be the best of the National Parks when it comes to MTBing, but the Preseli sneak inside the boundary, and they are crossed by a seriously good trail that makes the area well worth at least one visit. The main route here is an absolute epic, starting in the seaside town of Newport and clambering up onto the hills via a series of bridleways and narrow lanes. Once up, the main trail, known as the Golden Road after its one-time trade route status, runs for over 10km along the ridge top – a rollercoaster mix of scintillating singletrack and faint, boggy hollows. When it's good, it's very, very good, but there are one or two very short sections that can be slow and frustrating, especially during wetter periods. The trail rubs shoulders with some of the most spectacular tors, including Carn Menyn, famous for its involvement with Stonehenge, and it also offers amazing views across the rest of the range as well as of the coast and the ocean.

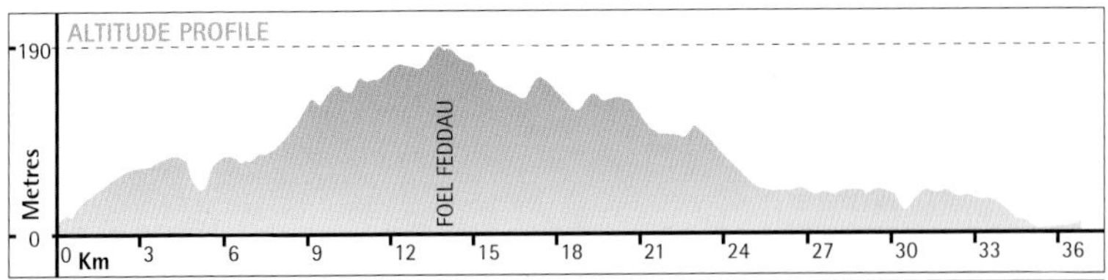

PRESELI HILLS – PEMBROKESHIRE **GRADE: ▲**

TOTAL DISTANCE: 37KM » **TOTAL ASCENT**: 880M » **TIME**: 4–5 HOURS » **START/FINISH**: NEWPORT
START GRID REF: SN 056392 » **SATNAV**: SA42 0TN » **OS MAP**: EXPLORER OL35; LANDRANGER 145
PUB: ROYAL OAK INN, NEWPORT, TEL: 01239 820 632 » **CAFÉ**: BLAS AT FRONLAS, NEWPORT

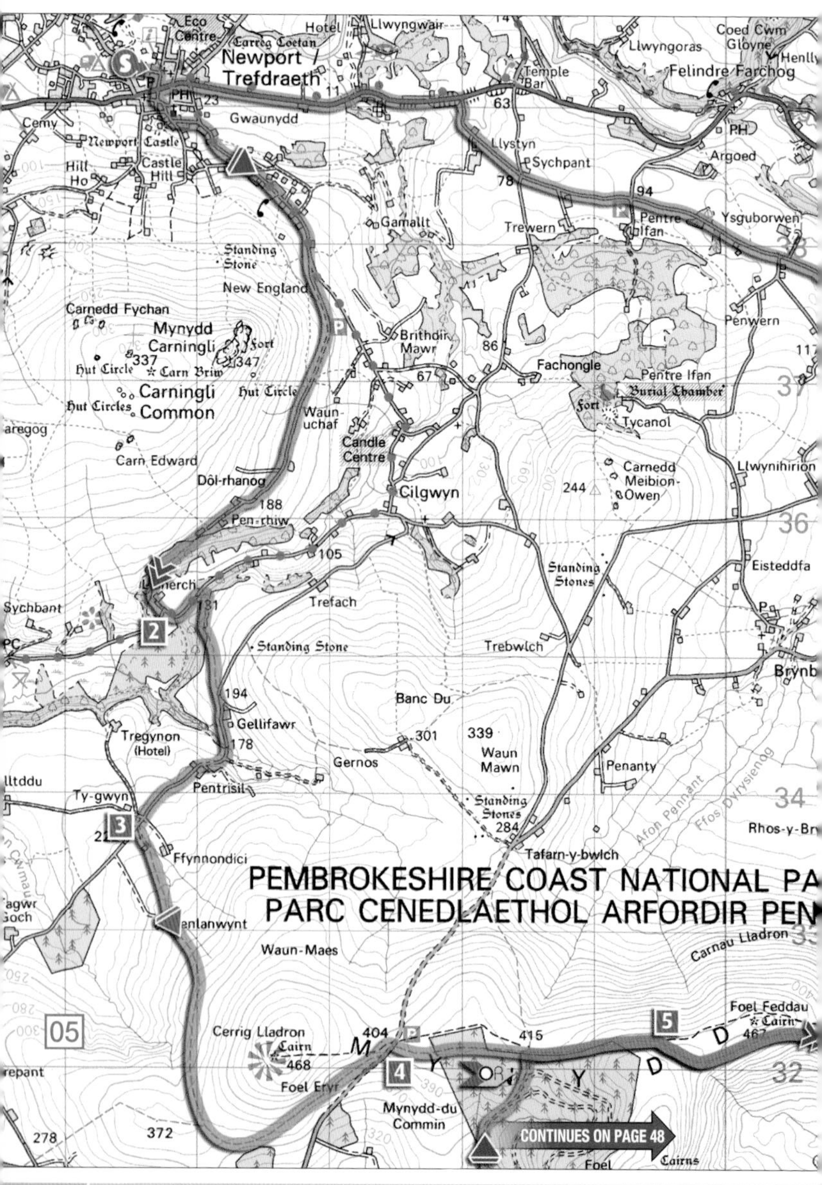
Eco Centre
Hotel
Llwyngwair
Carreg Coetan
Newport / Trefdraeth
Temple Bar
Llwyngoras
Coed Cwm Gloyne
Felindre Farchog
Henllys
PH
23
11
63
Cemy
Newport Castle
Gwaunydd
Llystyn
Sychpant
Argoed
Hill Ho
Castle Hill
78
94
Gamallt
Trewern
Pentre Ifan
Ysguborwen
Standing Stone
New England
Carnedd Fychan
Mynydd Carningli
Fort
337
347
Hut Circle
Carn Briw
Carningli Common
Hut Circles
Brithdir Mawr
86
67
Fachongle
Pentre Ifan
Burial Chamber
Penwern
Fort
Tycanol
37
Waun-uchaf
Candle Centre
Carn Edward
Dôl-rhanog
188
Cilgwyn
Carnedd Meibion-Owen
244
Llwynihirion
Pen-rhiw
105
36
Llannerch
Standing Stones
Eisteddfa
Sychbant
131
Trefach
2
Standing Stone
Trebwlch
Brynberian
194
Banc Du
Gellifawr
Tregynon (Hotel)
178
301
339
Gernos
Waun Mawn
Penanty
Pentrisil
Ty-gwyn
Standing Stones
284
Afon Pennant
Ffos Dyrysienog
34
Rhos-y-Bryn
3
Ffynnondici
Tafarn-y-bwlch
PEMBROKESHIRE COAST NATIONAL PARK
PARC CENEDLAETHOL ARFORDIR PENFRO
Waun-Maes
Carnau Lladron
Foel Feddau
Cairn
Cerrig Lladron
Cairn
468
404
415
5
05
M Y N Y D D
4
Foel Eryr
Mynydd-du Commin
32
278
372
CONTINUES ON PAGE 48
Foel
Cairns

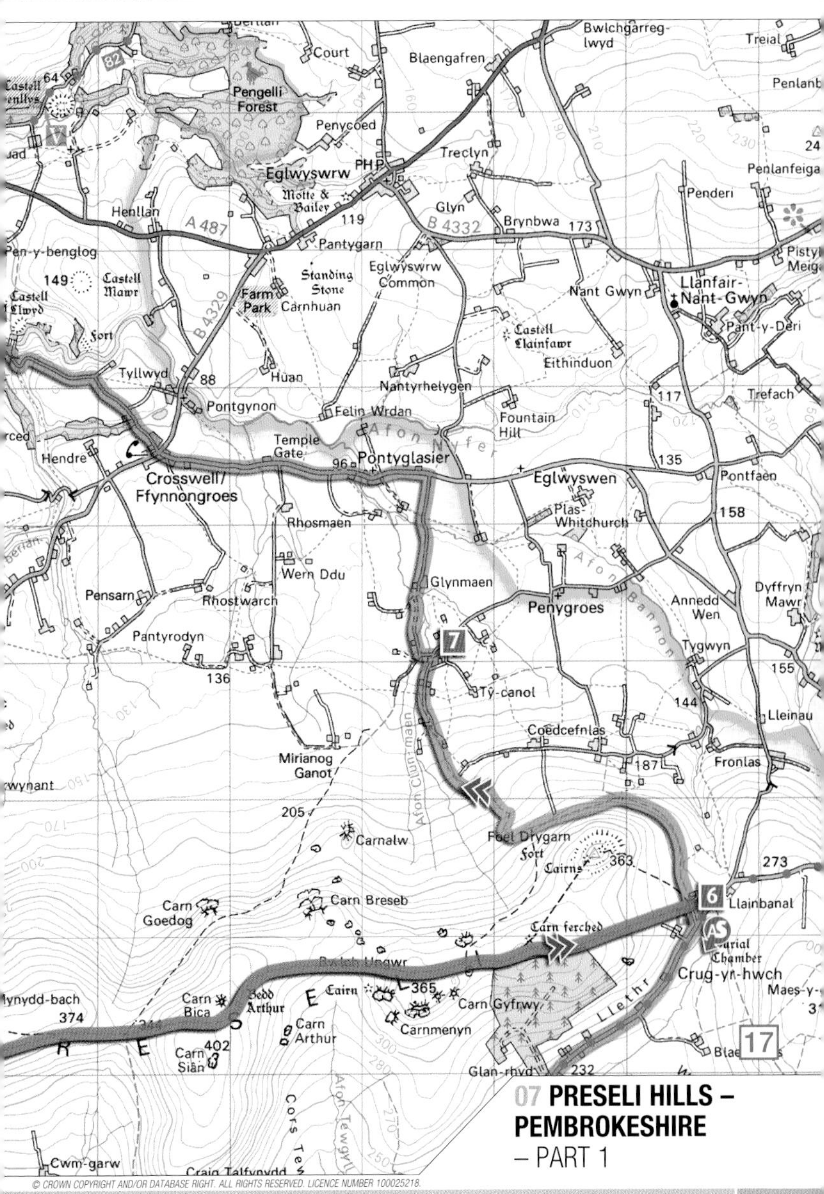

07 PRESELI HILLS – PEMBROKESHIRE – PART 1

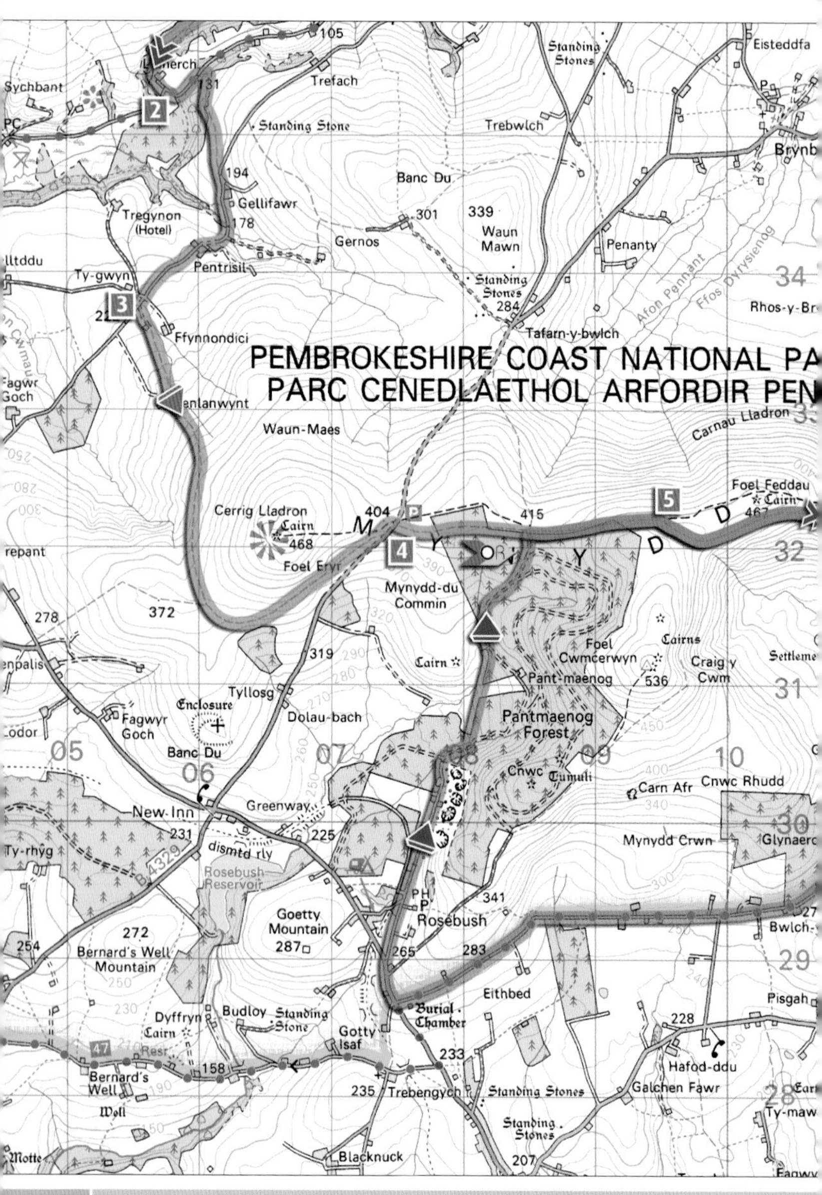
PEMBROKESHIRE COAST NATIONAL PA
PARC CENEDLAETHOL ARFORDIR PEN
Sychbant
Trefach
Standing Stone
Trebwlch
Standing Stones
Eisteddfa
Brynb
Banc Du
Gellifawr
Tregynon (Hotel)
Gernos
Waun Mawn
Penanty
Pentrisil
Ty-gwyn
Ffynnondici
Tafarn-y-bwlch
Afon Pennant
Ffos Dyrysienog
Rhos-y-Br
Waun-Maes
Carnau Lladron
Cerrig Lladron
Cairn
Foel Eryr
Foel Feddau
Mynydd-du Commin
Foel Cwmcerwyn
Pant-maenog
Pantmaenog Forest
Craig y Cwm
Cairns
Tyllosg
Enclosure
Fagwyr Goch
Banc Du
Dolau-bach
Cnwc
Tumuli
Carn Afr
Cnwc Rhudd
New Inn
Greenway
dismtd rly
Rosebush Reservoir
Mynydd Crwn
Glynaerc
Goetty Mountain
Rosebush
Bwlch-
Bernard's Well Mountain
Eithbed
Burial Chamber
Pisgah
Dyffryn
Budloy
Standing Stone
Gotty Isaf
Bernard's Well
Trebengych
Standing Stones
Hafod-ddu
Galchen Fawr
Ty-maw
Blacknuck
Motte
Ty-rhyg
Lodor
Well

07 PRESELI HILLS – PEMBROKESHIRE – PART 2

Directions – Preseli Hills – Pembrokeshire

S Turn **R** out of the car park and keep **SA** at main road onto Castle Street. Go up the hill and turn **L** into Church Street. Pass the church and turn **L** at College Square to continue to another junction, where you keep **SA**. Continue uphill past some houses to a fork marked by a Cwm Gwaun sign. Bear **R** (dead end) and follow it to its end, where it becomes a stony track that drops through the wood to join tarmac again.

2 Keep **SA** and then bear **sharp L** for 200m to a bridleway on the **R**. Climb steeply up through the wood and then keep close to the right edge of two fields to a road. Turn **R** and drop to cross Pont Gelli-fawr before continuing for 500m, to a drive on the left. Ignore this one, but take the next **L**, a rough track, after 100m.

3 Climb past two farms and continue alongside a wall to a tall fingerpost. Follow the line of the bridleway diagonally up to another post and continue in the same direction to a third. Stay with the posts until you meet a good singletrack that traverses around the hillside. Turn **R** onto this and follow it all the way out to the road – it is quite faint in places but as long as you don't gain any height, you can't go wrong, and it eventually establishes itself well.

4 Turn **L** onto the road and then turn immediately **R** onto another clear track. Follow this to a corner of the wood on the **R** and then bear diagonally **R**, across a boggy section, to join a clear track that continues, still quite boggy in places, along the line of the fence.

5 Stay with this now as it heads east for almost 10km, rising and dropping many times. Keep ahead at any junctions and aim to stay as close to the top of the ridge as possible. When you meet another wood on your right, and see an obvious rocky summit to your left, Foel Drygarn, you know you're nearing the end. Descend easily to a junction with a sunken track.

6 Turn **L** onto this and follow it around the hillside, ignoring any tracks off to the right. Keep **L** (high) after 1km and continue around the wall again until you reach its end. Now follow it around to the **R**, staying as close to the wall as you can to drop across some boggy ground, covered in gorse. Keep heading downhill until, at a farm, it becomes a drive. Follow this easily to the road.

7 Bear **L** to follow this to a T-junction with another lane and turn **L** to follow this to the B4329 at Crosswell. Keep **SA** to continue on narrow lanes that eventually drop to the A487. Turn **L** onto this and continue easily back into Newport.

Optional Shorter Route (25km, 520m ascent, 2–3 hours)

Start at the lay-by at SN075295 and turn **L** onto the road to ride through Mynachlog-ddu. Turn **R** on the outskirts of the village (signed *Rosebush*) and follow this to the B4313. Turn **R** onto this and **R** again into Rosebush then head up the small lane that runs north out of the village. Pass a slate quarry and keep **SA** through a gate before curving around to the right. Continue to a major fork and bear **L**. Now drop past a cottage, before climbing again with a valley to your left. Continue, keeping **L** at two forks to a gate and open moorland.

Turn **R**, joining midway through point **4**, and follow the main route to point **6**, where you turn **R** to return to the lay-by.

At a mere 230 square miles, Pembrokeshire is Britain's smallest National Park.

Making a weekend of it

This isn't a great area for mountain biking, although it's a great area for anything else including watersports and just chilling. The closest top-notch riding is really the trail centre at Brechfa Forest, or head back east and have a go at the **Gower** route (page 39)

HUGE VIEWS FROM THE MAIN PRESELI RIDGE

SECTION 2

Mid Wales

There's a truly wild feeling to the moors and mountains that make up the heart of Wales, and fortunately they are criss-crossed with some wonderful trails. Could MTBing get any better than this...

STEEP AND TECHNICAL IN THE IRFON FOREST (ROUTE 9)

CABAN-COCH RESERVOIR, ELAN VALLEY (ROUTE 11)

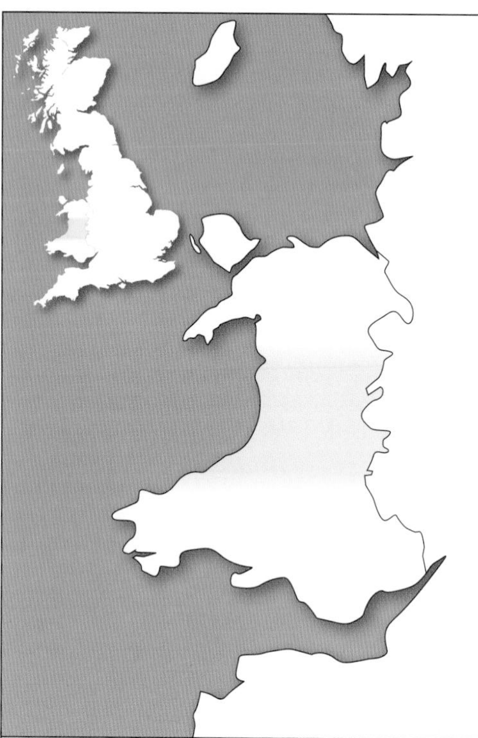

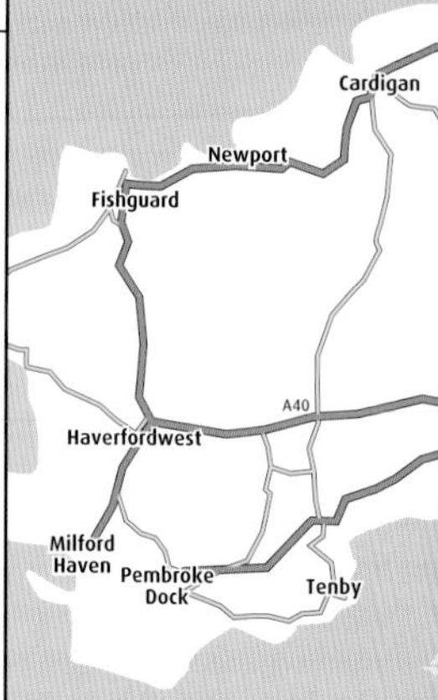

Mid Wales
route finder

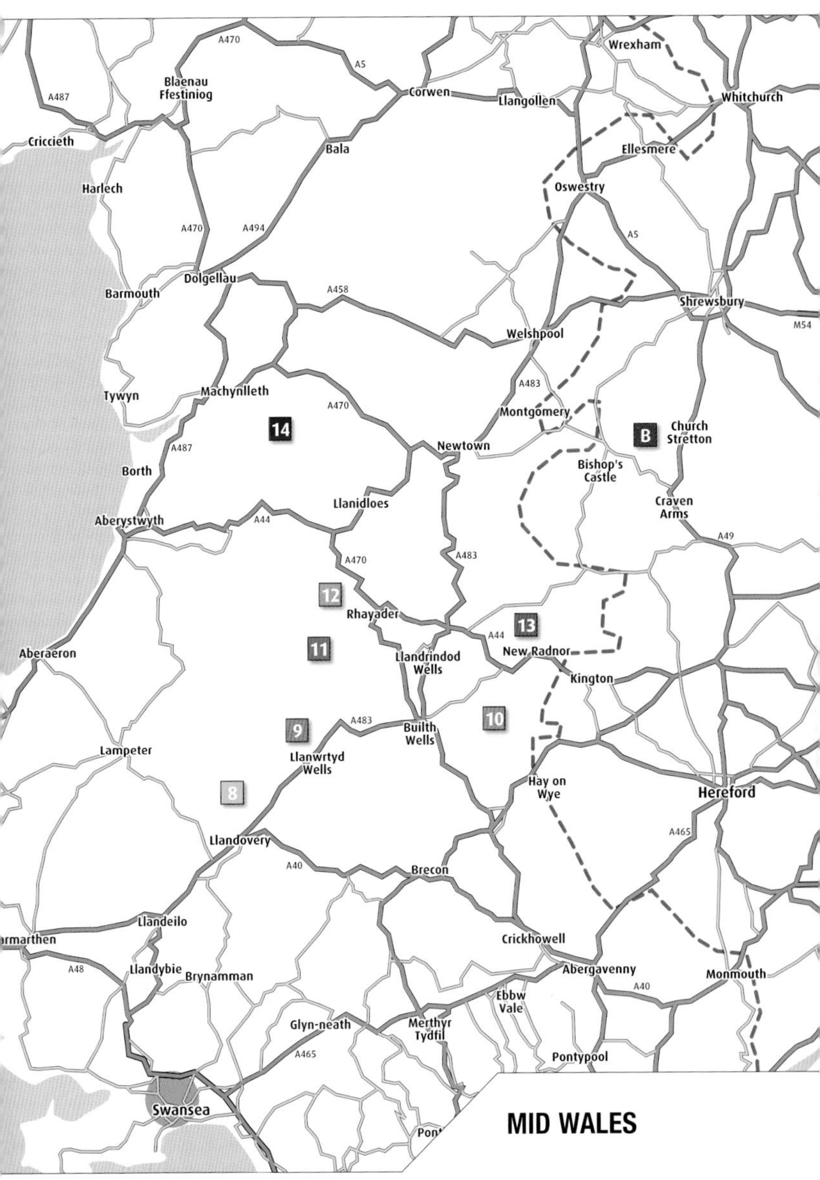
A470
A5
A487
Blaenau Ffestiniog
Corwen
Llangollen
Wrexham
Whitchurch
Criccieth
Bala
Ellesmere
Harlech
Oswestry
A470
A494
A5
Dolgellau
Barmouth
A458
Shrewsbury
M54
Welshpool
Tywyn
Machynlleth
A483
A470
Montgomery
14
B
Church Stretton
A487
Newtown
Borth
Bishop's Castle
Llanidloes
Craven Arms
Aberystwyth
A44
A49
A470
A483
12
Rhayader
13
A44
11
Aberaeron
Llandrindod Wells
New Radnor
Kington
A483
9
Builth Wells
10
Lampeter
Llanwrtyd Wells
Hay on Wye
8
Hereford
A465
Llandovery
A40
Brecon
Llandeilo
rmarthen
Crickhowell
A48
Llandybie
Brynamman
Abergavenny
A40
Monmouth
Ebbw Vale
Glyn-neath
Merthyr Tydfil
A465
Pontypool
Swansea
Pont

MID WALES

SPECTACULAR SCENERY NEAR SOAR Y MYNYDD

08 The Doethie Valley – Llandovery 23km

Introduction

The Afon Doethie rises up on a boggy plateau close to the Carmarthenshire/ Ceredigion border, right in the very remote heart of Mid Wales. Its two tributaries, the Doethie Fawr (Great Doethie) and Doethie Fach (Lesser Doethie), converge close to the wonderful remote hostel of Ty'n-y-cornel, and from there the tumbling river enjoys just a short life before being swallowed up by the Afon Towy, just a few miles north of Llandovery. Amazingly, during that short life, this wonderful river manages to carve itself one of the most stunningly scenic valleys in all of Wales. This ride exploits a bridleway that runs pretty much its full length.

The Ride

Although there's quite a lot to this little loop, the real substance is in the magnificent singletrack descent that runs down the Doethie Valley, which in places is as good, or even better, than anything else in Wales – natural or trail centre. The ride starts with an easy warm up on forest tracks, but height is being bagged all the time and by the time the trees give way to open hillside, it's a full-speed-ahead descent to the tiny church at Soar y Mynydd. Next up comes the toughest climb of the day – if you make it over the first section without footing then you truly are among the elite. From here, we cruise across the top of the moor before an exciting and rough descent, but don't get too carried away; there's a turning to look for and it's easily missed. Now it's singletrack down to the valley path, and more of it down the valley itself. The highlight has to be the short rocky section – straight out of Indiana Jones. From the bottom it's another climb, and then a short, sharp drop down to the finish.

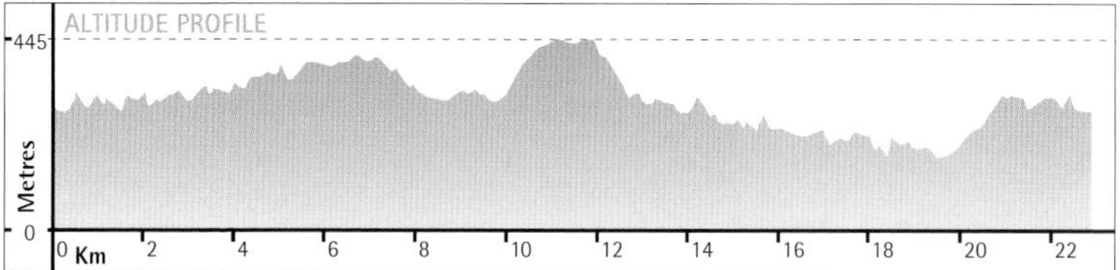

THE DOETHIE VALLEY – LLANDOVERY **GRADE: ▲**

TOTAL DISTANCE: 23KM » **TOTAL ASCENT**: 1130M » **TIME**: 3-4 HOURS » **START/FINISH**: LLYN BRIANNE
START GRID REF: SN 793484 » **SATNAV**: RHANDIRMWYN (NEAREST) » **OS MAP**: EXPLORER 187; LANDRANGER 147
PUB: THE TOWY BRIDGE INN, TOWY BRIDGE, TEL: 01550 760 370; THE ROYAL OAK, RHANDIRMWYN, TEL: 01550 760 201
CAFÉ: OFTEN A SNACK VAN AT THE START

Directions – Doethie Valley – Llandovery

S Cross the dam and follow the main gravel track around the lake, taking two sharp right-hand bends and then veering around to the left. Stay on the main track, ignoring a turning to the left, and drop to another sharp right-hand bend, where you **ignore** a right fork and climb, still on the main track, around a small summit. Swing **L** again and ignore another right-hand turn before crossing some open ground. Veer **sharp R** at another fork and then drop all the way down to the chapel at Soar y Mynydd.

2 Take the first **L** onto a steep and loose track and climb up onto moorland. Continue for 2km before dropping steeply into the next valley. Look for a waymarked bridleway on the **L** (easily missed) and go through a gate to drop down into the Doethie Valley.

3 Bear **L** to follow the track down the valley, keeping **L** at an obvious saddle, with a small hill ahead. Continue to a clearer track by a ruin. Continue down the valley without deviating at all. You'll pass a particularly narrow section and then climb away from the river slightly to continue through woodland. Keep **SA** and eventually you'll merge with a good farm track.

4 Keep **L** to the farmyard and pass through two gates. Take a gravel track on the **L** and climb for some distance to the top. Keep **SA** to drop through a gate, and down to a T-junction. Turn **R** to retrace your earlier tracks back to the Dam.

Pronunciation - Doethie: **Doy-thi-uh**

Making a day of it

There's not a lot that could be easily added to this one, but there are forest tracks leading west towards Abergwesyn and the **Irfon Forest** route (page 63).

Making a weekend of it

The obvious choice would the **Irfon Forest** route (page 63) but you're not too far from some of the Brecon Beacons routes here too. It's also not too much of a stretch to tie in a day at Brechfa or Coed Trallwm, if you fancy a little trail centre action.

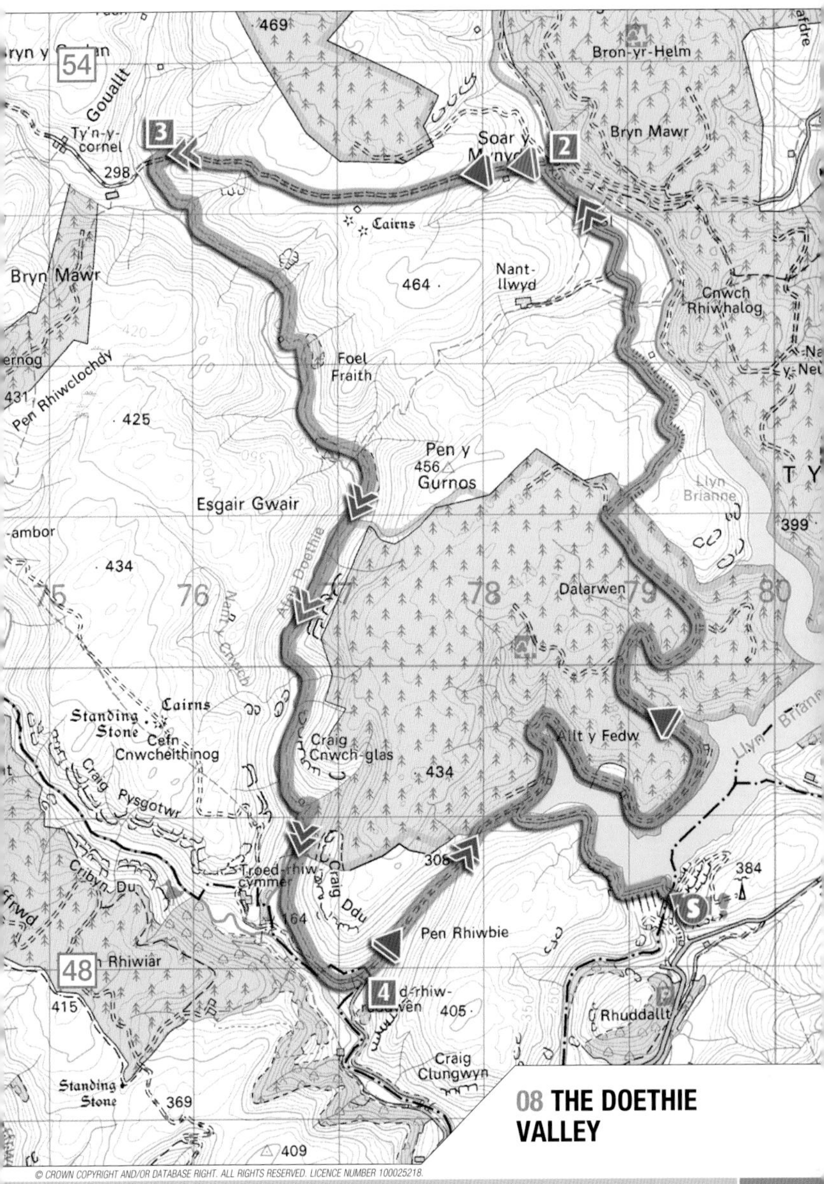
08 THE DOETHIE VALLEY

HIDDEN SINGLETRACK IN THE FOREST

09 Irfon Forest – Llanwrtyd Wells 23km

Introduction

Llanwrtyd Wells is famous for being Britain's smallest town – a dubious honour that's somewhat difficult to quantify. It's also developed a reputation for all kinds of extreme and whacky sports including the Man versus Horse race and the World Bog Snorkelling Championships. Smallest or not, it's a lovely little place, with a tidy main street decorated with an impressive statue of a red kite (the mountains north of the town were the final refuge of this wonderful raptor before the reintroduction program returned their numbers to the healthy levels we see now). It's set among some wonderfully scenic upland countryside, with the Irfon Forest stretching north from its streets.

The Ride

23km doesn't seem like a lot for a hard route, but with nearly 1,000m of ascent, this little gem will test even the best. It's a wonderfully mixed bag with most of the climbing done on rocky tracks or forest roads, and the descents providing plenty of variety as well as exhilaration. The best of the descents is the first one, a wonderful stretch of natural singletrack that drops from high in the forest to the banks of the Afon Irfon. The top feels like an abstract section of crazy paving cut from dark, slatey rock that steepens with almost every metre, and the bottom links a number of stream-cut steps that only the bravest will clean. There's more singletrack later on, the first section tight and narrow though the trees, and the second, seriously steep and exposed enough to make anyone think twice before committing; but there's also some good fast blasts too, and more than the odd boggy patch to slow things down. The final drop comes with a huge grin factor, as do the pubs and teashops in town.

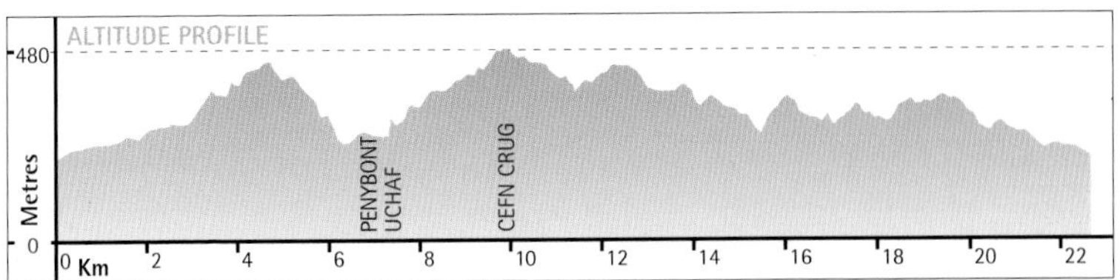

IRFON FOREST – LLANWRTYD WELLS **GRADE:** ▲

TOTAL DISTANCE: 23KM » **TOTAL ASCENT**: 960M » **TIME**: 3-4 HOURS » **START/FINISH**: LLANWRTYD WELLS
START GRID REF: SN 878467 » **SATNAV**: LD5 4RB » **OS MAP**: OS EXPLORER 200; LANDRANGER 147 » **PUB**: THE NUEADD ARMS HOTEL, LLANWRTYD WELLS, TEL: 01591 610 236 » **CAFÉ**: THE DROVERS REST, LLANWRTYD WELLS, TEL: 01591 610 264

OUT OF THE WOODS BUT STILL ON SINGLETRACK

09 IRFON FOREST –
LLANWRTYD WELLS
LLANWRTYD WELLS /
LLANWRTUD
Irfon Forest
Cefn Pen-y-bont
Crugwydd
Pen Disgwylfa
Cefn Waun-lwyd
Cefn Blaeneinon
Bwlchmawr
Pen y Garn-goch
Pistyllgwyn
Penfedw
Ffosyrhyddod
Gilfach
Penhenwernfach
Woollen Mill
Garn Dwad
Pen-y-banc
Cefn Alltwinau
Alltwineu
Penybont Uchaf
Pen y Ddinas
Llanwrtyd
Dinas Mill
Kilsby
Cemy Hotel
Victoria Wells
Henfron
Henbant
Penmaenllwyd
Llwyneuadd
Ty'n-y-maes
Bryn
Allt-y-gest
Garn Wen
Banc Paderau
Tynypant
Bronffynnon
Penrhiwgoc
Llawes-heli
Ffos Fm
Hotel
A 483

Directions – Irfon Forest – Llanwrtyd Wells

S Head north-east out of town on the A483 (cycle lane) to the first turning on the **L** and follow this to its end by a house. Continue on a rough track that leads into the forest and bear **L** to start climbing. Continue until it levels and then descends for 300m, and take a rough track on the **L**.

2 Follow this steep slickrock descent to a crossroads and keep **SA** to continue through the forest and out onto pasture, where you keep **SA** to the bottom and then turn **R** to **walk through the yard** of Penybont Uchaf. Turn **R** onto the road to the Pwll y Bo Picnic Area.

3 Turn **R** into the car park and go through a gate to take the higher track up into the woods. Stay with this, **ignore** one track on the right, and then one on the left, then two more on the right. Eventually you'll round a hairpin bend and continue to climb until you reach level ground, where a good track comes in from the right.

4 Continue past this for 200m and then look for a very faint track to the **R** (**easy to miss**). Take this, which quickly improves, and descend to a forest track. Turn **L** and then **R** to descend around sharp bends and over a stream. Climb away and continue for 1km to a sharp left-hand bend. Immediately after this, bear **R** onto another track.

5 Follow this to a right-hand bend and keep **SA** onto a grassy track that leaves the forest and crosses open ground to a gate. Keep **SA** to climb on a grassy track around the top of Cribyn Bedw and keep ahead to descend to a gate. Continue in the same direction eventually following a faint track along the edge of field to a gate directly ahead.

6 Don't go through but bear **R**, through a bridlegate, onto a very steep section of singletrack. Follow this down to a stream and climb away to two gates at the top. Take the gate on the **R** to continue climbing on a fenced track that vaults a hilltop before descending to a gate on the **L**, immediately before it starts climbing again.

7 Go through the gate and drop steeply down the edge of the field to a ford. Cross this and climb away to continue past a house to a drive. Follow this **L** to join another drive and turn **L** onto this to drop to a farmyard. Turn **R** onto tarmac and continue to a remote farm.

8 Keep **SA** to climb and drop and then, at the bottom, keep **L** to climb again. Continue to a fork by a gate on the right. Don't go through but keep high through another gate, and continue **SA** on a variety of surfaces until you round a sharp right-hand bend close to a house. Continue around the house and through a gate that leads to the Woollen Mill. Turn **R** onto the A483 to return to Llanwrtyd Wells.

Remember the '**f**' in Irfon is pronounced as a '**v**.'

Making a day of it

The easiest extension would be west from Abergwesyn to the shores of Llyn Brianne, where this route could be linked with the **Doethie Valley** loop (page 59). This would be a **big** day.

Making a weekend of it

The **Doethie Valley** route (page 59) is within sensible reach; and the **Elan Valley** loops (pages 75 and 81) aren't too far either. There are also some man-made trails at Coed Trallwm, just down the road.

EASY GOING ON LLANBEDR HILL

10 Llanbedr Hill – Border Country 37km

Introduction

The upland region east of Builth Wells and north of Hay-on-Wye seems to fall off the radar for most visitors to Wales, which is a shame as it's a wonderfully remote area, despite the close proximity of the English border. It's also incredibly scenic, with tall, heather-covered hilltops and deeply cloven valleys. Nature abounds here; kites and buzzards omnipresent in the skies, and red grouse and many other moorland birds grazing on the tops. It's also full of historical interest including some long and very distinct sections of Offa's Dyke, and some quite interesting burial cairns and graves. Two of these are visited in this ride.

The Ride

A four up, four down marathon with enough climbing to wear most MTBers out, and some wonderful descents that will ensure everyone finishes with a smile on their face. The opener is definitely doable, courtesy of mainly good surfaces, and that rewards with some great switchbacks to the Cwmblaenerw Brook. The next one, from the Afon Edw onto Llandeilo Hill is bigger and tougher, and few will manage this one without a push. But it leads to a lovely cruisey section over onto Llanbedr Hill that ends with a sweet drop down to the Bachawy Brook. It's short and sharp onto Allt Dderw from here; and then it's fast and furious down again. This leaves one final pull, and it's a long one too – just what the doctor ordered after a long ride. But from the Giant's Grave, gravity is well and truly on the right team, and the final kilometres will fly by in a blur of grass, gravel and finally tarmac.

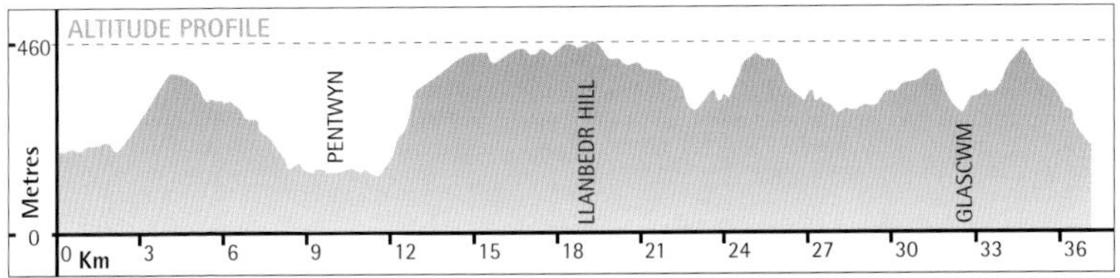

LLANBEDR HILL – BORDER COUNTRY **GRADE: ▲**

TOTAL DISTANCE: 37KM » **TOTAL ASCENT**: 1,270M » **TIME**: 4.5–6 HOURS » **START/FINISH**: HUNDRED HOUSE
START GRID REF: SO 112544 » **SATNAV**: LD1 5RY (NEAREST) » **OS MAP**: EXPLORER 188, 200; LANDRANGER 147, 148
PUB: SEVEN STARS INN, ABEREDW, TEL: 01982 560 494 » **CAFÉ**: NONE

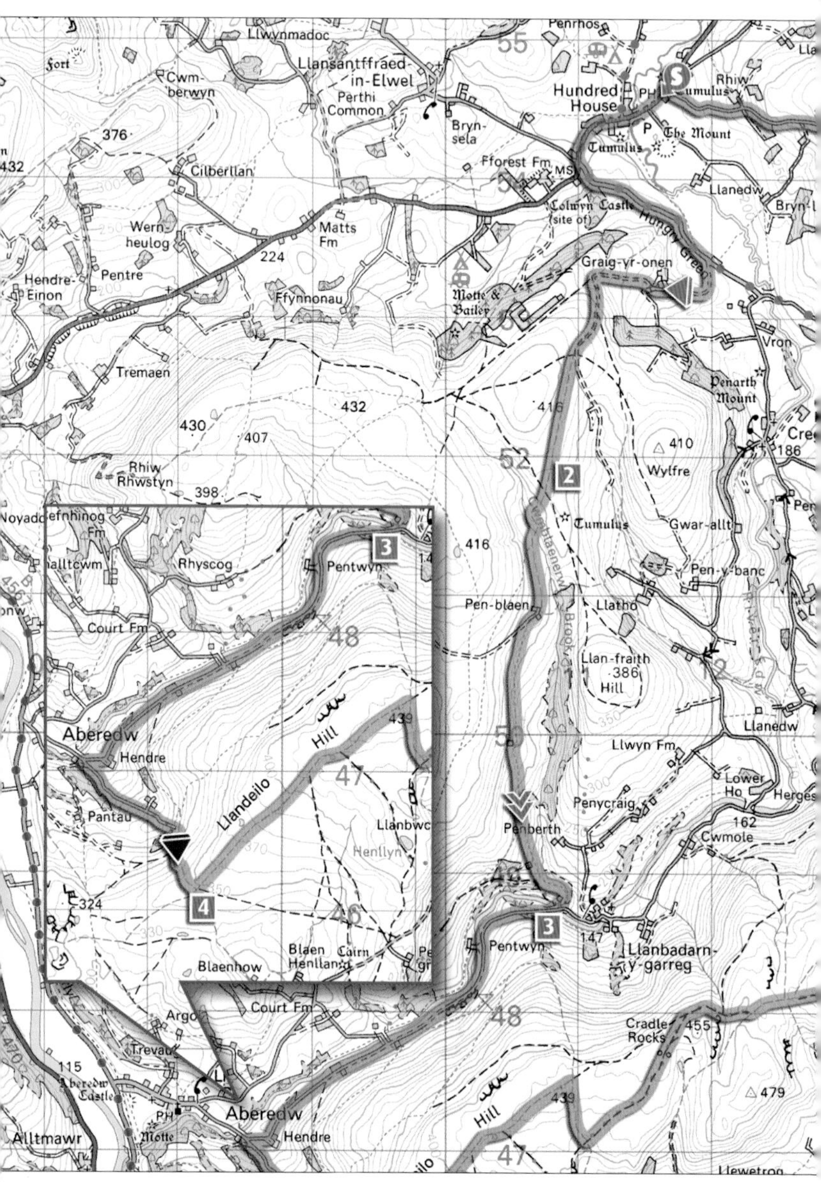

Llwynmadoc
Llansantffraed-in-Elwel
Perthi Common
Cwm-berwyn
Hundred House
The Mount
Cilberllan
Fforest Fm
Colwyn Castle (site of)
Wern-heulog
Matts Fm
Hungry Green
Hendre-Einon
Pentre
Ffynnonau
Graig-yr-onen
Motte & Bailey
Tremaen
Vron
Penarth Mount
Rhiw Rhwstyn
Wylfre
Tumulus
Gwar-allt
Pentwyn
Rhyscog
Court Fm
Pen-y-banc
Pen-blaen
Llatho
Llan-fraith Hill
Aberedw
Hendre
Llandeilo Hill
Llanedw
Llwyn Fm
Pantau
Llanbwch
Henllyn
Lower Ho
Penycraig
Penberth
Cwmole
Blaen Henllan
Cairn
Blaenhow
Llanbadarn-y-garreg
Cradle Rocks
Trevaur
Aberedw Castle
Motte
Alltmawr

10 LLANBEDR HILL – BORDER COUNTRY

Directions – Llanbedr Hill – Border Country

S Turn **R** out of the car park and then first **L** (Glasgwm). Turn **R** onto a drive after 1km and follow this up past a farm on the right to a gate, where you turn **L** to continue on the main track. At the top, fork **R** onto a duplex track and follow this to another fork, where you turn **R** onto a grassy trail.

2 This drops to cross the Cwmblaenerw Brook. Climb out and bear **L** to follow the valley down, **ignoring** a right fork, to a gate that leads onto a farm track. Follow this down to a barn, where you head up onto a drive and then immediately **L** to follow a sunken track down. Keep **SA** on this vague trail and pass other derelict buildings before it eventually improves and drops to the road.

3 Turn **R** and follow the road along the valley floor for 3km to Hendre Farm. Shortly after this, turn **L** onto a steep lane (straight ahead to Aberedw village and the pub). Climb steeply onto dirt, and keep ahead to a gate that leads onto open hillside. Keep ahead for a few metres and then turn **sharp R** – almost back on yourself – and continue climbing with power lines to your right. Continue **SA** at a crossroads to the top.

4 Turn **L** onto a good track that follows the ridge top, and continue climbing gradually past a pool on your right to Twm Tobacco's Grave. Bear **R** here (straight ahead is not legal) onto a vague track through the heather, and continue to a good track, where you turn **L**. Follow this to a junction with the original track and keep ahead to the road at Ireland.

5 Turn **R** and then immediately **L** onto a grassy track, keeping the field on your left, and now follow the main track for 2km to a junction at a field corner. Turn **L** to drop towards a gate and then turn **L** onto a drive that bends right and drops to a farm. Keep **SA** on a rough track that drops to the road and turn **L** and then **R**.

6 Climb past a farm on the left and continue **SA** to a drive to the right. Turn **R** here and follow this down to a remote farmhouse and keep **SA** to follow a clear track that climbs out onto open hillside. Keep **SA** to a crossroads with a broad, rutted track and turn **R**. Follow this for nearly 2km to a road at a hairpin bend.

7 Turn **L** to drop to a left-hand bend, where you keep **SA**, through a gate, to climb and then drop to a road. Turn **L** for 1km, then **L** again. Continue to a crossroads and turn **L** towards Glasgwm. Climb, then drop, into the village and turn **R** in the centre to drop to a left-hand bend, where you keep **SA** (dead end).

8 Climb on a good track that passes a farm down to the left, before dropping to cross the valley floor. Stay on the track to climb away from this and over a high pass. Drop to a good track and follow it down to the road. Keep **SA** on the road to drop to the A481, where you turn **L** to the finish.

Twm Tobacco was a 17th century Jack the Lad, involved in everything from sheep rustling to selling tobacco. He died on Llanbedr Hill.

Making a day of it

This is quite a big loop already but it could be extended by continuing east and hooking up with the trails that run over and around Hergest Ridge.

Making a weekend of it

Both the **Elan Valley** (pages 75 and 81) and the **Irfon Forest** route (page 63) are within easy reach of this route. And there's also the trail centre at Coed Trallwm.

SLATEY TRAILS IN THE SHORT FOREST SECTION

11 Claerwen Valley – Elan Valley

12km

Introduction

The Claerwen Reservoir is the highest of the Elan Valley reservoirs, and was also the last to be built, only opening in 1952. It's a huge construction, over 50m high and 350m long, yet it's quite impressive to look at, mainly because it's clad with local stone, despite being actually constructed with concrete. Between the huge dam and the lower Caban-coch Reservoir, 5km downstream, lies the lower Claerwen Valley, a typical mid Wales dale complete with steep and rugged sides and a cascading river running through its heart. The road to the dam hogs the valley floor to the north of the river, but it's the trail on the south bank that forms the basis for this route.

The Ride

This is one of the shortest and easiest routes in the book, and as such makes a great introduction to mid Wales riding. The outward leg hops over the Afon Claerwen near its confluence with the Caban-coch Reservoir and climbs easily up onto a broad trail that traverses the steep southern banks. It's a bit rough and ready in places, but it also makes for some great rollercoaster riding, with no huge ups or downs to break the flow. At the foot of the dam, there's a river to cross; most will opt for the short walk and the footbridge rather than the ford, which comes with a guarantee of wet feet. It's worth climbing up to see the dam, even if it does mean a steep drop back down again afterwards. The second leg starts with a steep climb out of the valley and continues, after a simple crossing of the 438m Rhos Gelynnen, with a manic plummet back down through the forest on a bed of pine needles and the odd patch of slippery slate. A narrow waterside road returns to the car park.

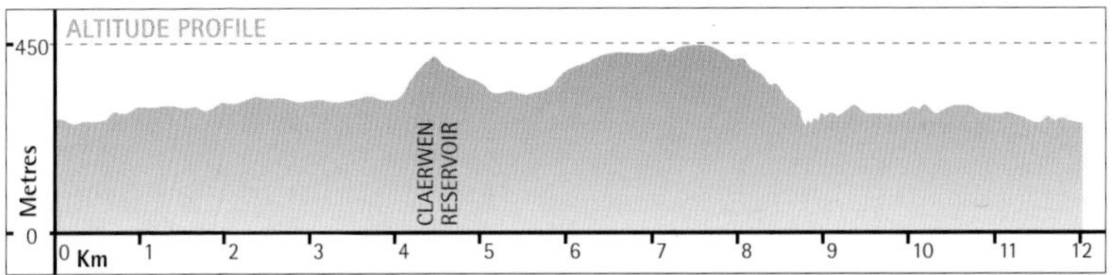

CLAERWEN VALLEY – ELAN VALLEY **GRADE: ▲**

TOTAL DISTANCE: 12KM » **TOTAL ASCENT**: 440M » **TIME**: 1–2 HOURS » **START/FINISH**: CLAERWEN VALLEY
START GRID REF: SN 900616 » **SATNAV**: ELAN VILLAGE (NEAREST) » **OS MAP**: EXPLORER 200; LANDRANGER 147
PUB: NONE NEARBY » **CAFÉ**: THE ELAN VALLEY VISITOR CENTRE, ELAN VILLAGE, TEL: 01597 810 880; OTHER OPTIONS IN RHAYADER

THE CLAERWEN DAM

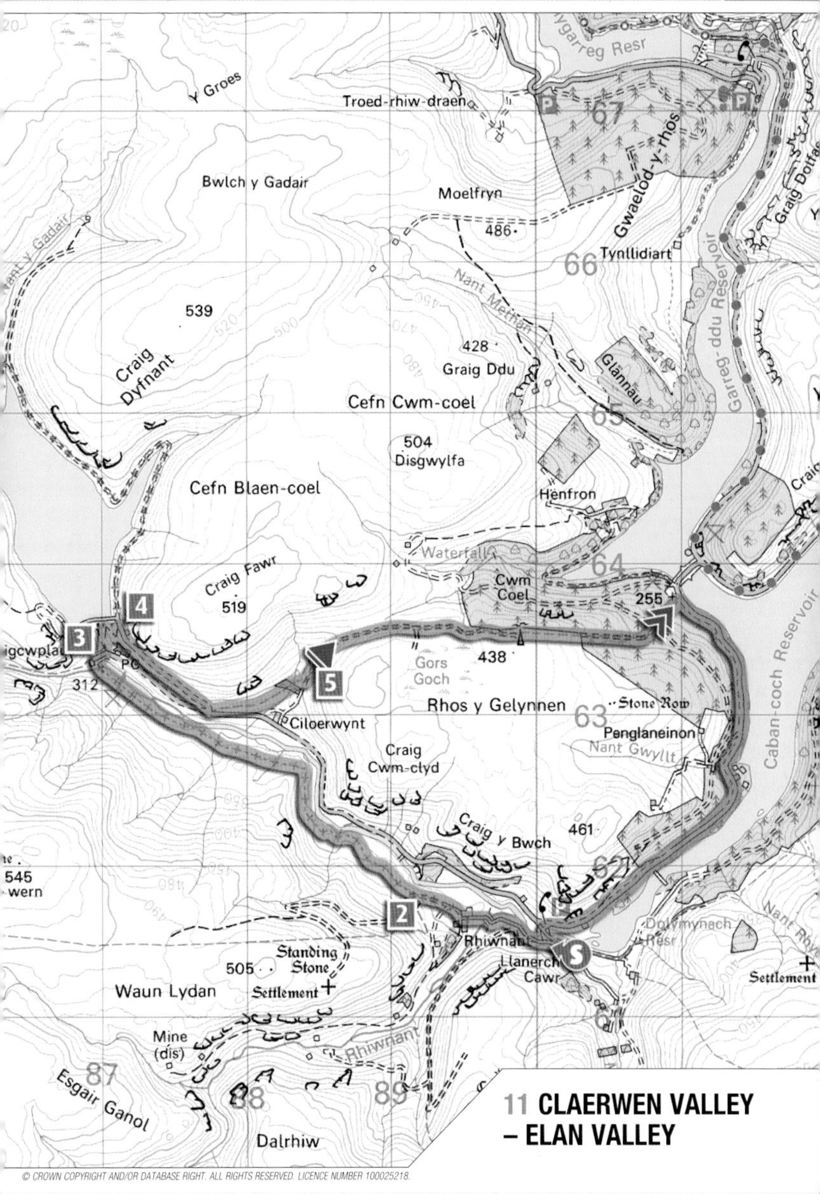
Y Groes
Troed-rhiw-draen
Bwlch y Gadair
Moelfryn
486
Gwaelod-y-rhos
Tynllidiart
539
Craig Dyfnant
428
Graig Ddu
Cefn Cwm-coel
Glannau
504
Disgwylfa
Cefn Blaen-coel
Henfron
Waterfall
Craig Fawr
519
Cwm Coel
255
438
Gors Goch
Rhos y Gelynnen
Stone Row
Ciloerwynt
312
Craig Cwm-clyd
Penglaneinon
Nant Gwyllt
Craig y Bwch
461
545
Rhiwnant
Standing Stone
505
Llanerch Cawr
Waun Lydan
Settlement
Mine (dis)
Rhiwnant
Esgair Ganol
Dalrhiw
Caban-coch Reservoir
Garreg-ddu Reservoir
Dolymynach Resr
Settlement
Nant Methan
Graig Dolfaen
11 CLAERWEN VALLEY – ELAN VALLEY

Directions – Claerwen Valley – Elan Valley

S Drop down past the telephone box to cross the rickety bridge over the Afon Claerwen. Continue uphill and **L** towards the farm buildings and then turn **sharp R** to follow a tarmac track above the river. Continue past a bridleway that forks left and cross the Rhiwnant River before reaching the Rhiwnant Farm. Keep **SA** here, with the river down to your right, and continue past a small plantation on the left before reaching a fork.

2 Fork **R** here and continue easily upstream for another 3km, with great views up the valley towards the Claerwen Dam and also across the river to the craggy ramparts that guard the featureless plateau of Rhos y Gelynnen. Eventually your way will be blocked by the Afon Arban. If the ford looks bad, there's a footbridge a few metres upstream but remember this is footpath **so please dismount**. Continue over the bridge over the Afon Claerwen, with the huge dam up above.

3 Look for a gate on the **L** of the plantation ahead, and go through this to climb steeply up to the road by the eastern tip of the dam. There are now fine views across the reservoir, to the remote rolling Cwmdeudwr Hills; and back down the Claerwen Valley.

4 Turn around and follow the road downhill to the junction with the bottom road. Turn **L** onto this, and then **L** again, onto a waymarked bridleway. Follow this steeply up and then continue as it flattens off and dips to cross a stream. Climb steeply up the bank opposite.

5 Turn **L** onto a good track. As this turns right, to go to the masts, keep **SA** to follow a grassy track downhill with the forest to your left. Go through a gate into the forest, and drop steeply, going **SA** at a crossroads, to join the road by the Carreg-ddu Viaduct. Turn **R** onto the road and enjoy an easy pootle past the Caban-coch Reservoir to the start.

The Elan Valley reservoirs were built during the late 19th century to provide water for Birmingham. They do this via a pipeline that runs for over 100km, yet drops by a mere 52m so that the water is moved by gravity alone.

Making a day of it

Follow the Elan Valley trail down to the Visitor Centre and continue through Elan Village before zigzagging southwards to the bridleway junction at SN 937638. From here, follow the bridleway back down to the bridge near the start. Alternatively, from the road at the finish, pick up the **Elan Valley Epic** (page 81) and mix and match your own extension loop.

Making a weekend of it

The obvious bundle is the **Elan Valley Epic** (page 81), but this is a tougher ride. Other alternatives include the **Irfon Forest** loop (page 63) or a visit to Coed Trallwm for trail centre singletrack.

THE MAGNIFICENT RED KITE

12 Elan Valley – Rhayader

30km

Introduction

Such was the size of the project of building the Elan Valley dams, that a railway needed to be laid just to carry materials, and a whole village was built to house the workers and their families. The village still stands, close to the visitor centre, and the railway now forms the basis for the Elan Valley Trail – a family cycle trail from Rhayader into the heart of the lakes. This route uses the car park for the Trail as a starting point but takes an altogether more strenuous overview of the area and its huge reservoirs by weaving a sinuous thread through the lofty whaleback hills that tower over the waterways.

The Ride

This is one of the most strenuous outings in the book, despite not being too long or actually involving too much ascent. It's the nature of the terrain that takes its toll, with most of the trails crossing ground that's either very steep or very rough. It starts with a long pull from Rhayader up onto Esgair Penygarreg, the route's highpoint and, at 533m, a wonderfully wild viewpoint. The descent, particularly down from Y Gurn, makes it all worthwhile – a mix of singletrack and duplex adorned with short rocky steps. Then it's another climb onto another airy viewpoint, this one high above the Carreg-ddu Reservoir. The descent that follows requires serious downhill ability and pads might not go a miss either; but the really rough bits are short-lived so mere mortals can walk them without feeling short-changed. A cruise around the reservoir follows, before the final climb onto Esgair Perfedd. From the top, it's grassy singletrack around to the road, and a short road section gains Penrhiw-wen for a rough and tumble 300m descent to Rhayader.

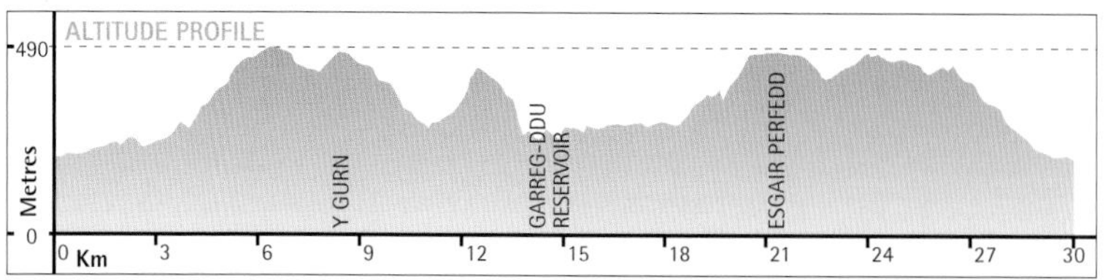

ELAN VALLEY – RHAYADER **GRADE: ▲**

TOTAL DISTANCE: 30KM » **TOTAL ASCENT**: 1,150M » **TIME**: 3-4 HOURS » **START/FINISH**: ELAN VALLEY TRAIL, RHAYADER **START GRID REF**: SN 965677 » **SATNAV**: RHAYADER » **OS MAP**: EXPLORER 200; LANDRANGER 147 » **PUB**: GOOD PUBS IN RHAYADER » **CAFÉ**: THE ELAN VALLEY VISITOR CENTRE, ELAN VILLAGE, TEL: 01597 810 880; OTHER OPTIONS IN RHAYADER

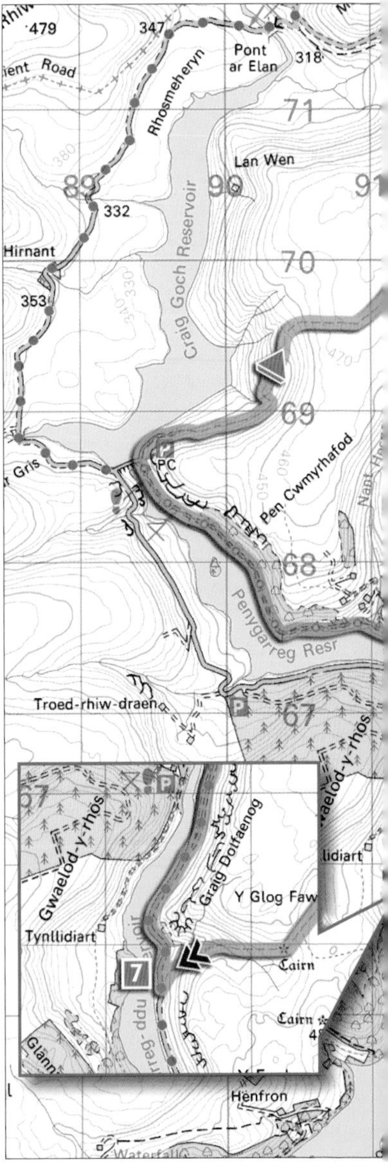
479
347
Pont ar Elan
318
Road
Rhosmeheryn
71
Lan Wen
380
89
90
91
332
Craig Goch Reservoir
Hirnant
70
353
340
330
470
69
Pen Cwmyrhafod
460
450
PC
68
Penygarreg Resr
Troed-rhiw-draen
67
Gwaelod-y-rhos
Craig Dolfaenog
Y Glog Faw
lidiart
Tynllidiart
7
Cairn
Glann
Hënfron
Waterfall

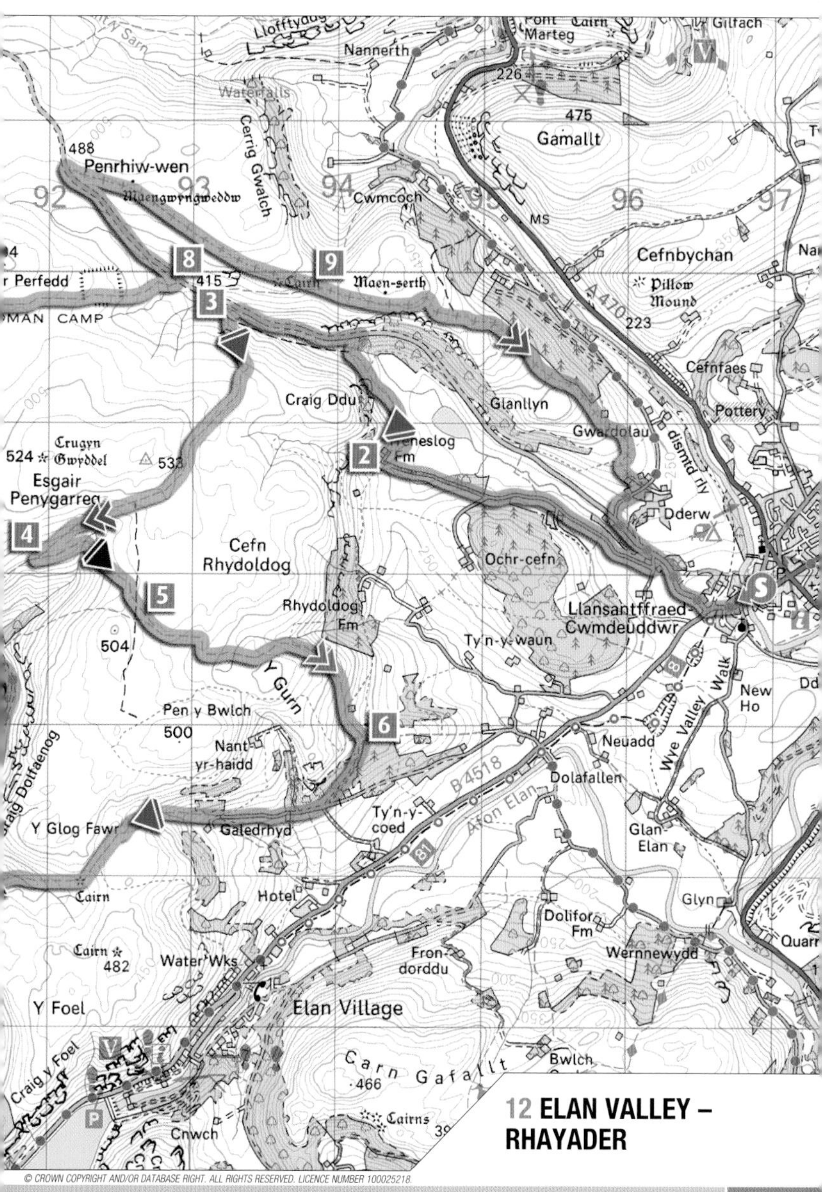

12 ELAN VALLEY – RHAYADER

Directions – Elan Valley – Rhayader

S Turn **R** out of the car park and **R** again (signed *Mountain Road to Aberystwyth*). Turn **L** after 500m and follow this around to the left then right and then climb steadily above pasture. Where the road swings left, keep **SA** on a farm drive and then turn **R** in front of the farm.

2 Go through a yard and a succession of gates onto a grassy track and follow this up and then down to a fork; turn **R** (waymark post) to drop to the stream. Cross this and climb to the road, where you turn **L**. Climb to the top of the hill to a clear track on the left (waymarked bridleway).

3 Turn **L**, drop down to cross the stream again and then bear **L** across a boggy section and pick up a stony track. Climb steeply to the top, where a waymark directs you **R**. Continue on a grassy track that climbs past the trig point, and then descends sweetly.

4 As the valley deepens to your left, keep an eye open for a very vague track on the **L** and follow this as it drops to cross the stream. Follow the grassy wall straight up from the stream and after 10 minutes of pushing, you'll meet the track you diverted from earlier.

5 Turn **R** for a few metres and then fork **L**, by a fenced off square, to climb past a boundary stone. Stay with track, which starts as really good singletrack but is interrupted by a bog, before continuing as really good singletrack again. Ford a stream and keep **L** at the fork immediately afterwards, then descend all the way down to a drive. Keep ahead to a crossroads of tracks above a wood.

6 Bear **R** onto a broad track and follow it to a road. Turn **R** and then fork **L** to continue past a cottage to a waymarked bridleway on the **R**. Follow the track over a stream and then climb up the valley, with the stream to your **R**. This leads to a good singletrack that drops to cross a stream. Keep **SA** to climb slightly, and then drop very steeply to the road.

7 Turn **R** and then fork **R** to climb above a wood. Keep **L** at the fork to drop slightly, and then follow the track past the dam and alongside the reservoir. Continue past the Craig Goch dam and climb steeply up the hillside. This becomes faint but stay with it as it improves near the top. Drop easily down to a ford and then climb back up to the road.

8 Turn **L** and climb for 1km to an obvious track on the **R**. Follow this down past turnings on the left and right and keep **SA** to climb slightly and then keep **R** to contour around Esgair Ddewr.

9 Now drop steeply down and continue alongside a wood. Follow the waymarks **L** then **R** to stay on the main byway and then follow the drive along the edge of the field to the road. Turn **R** and then **L** at the bottom. Drop to the B4518 and turn **L** to return to Rhayader.

Rhayader is actually spelt **Rhaeadr** in Welsh and means waterfall. The town is called Rhaeadr Gwy in Welsh as it is built on some falls on the River Wye (Afon Gwy).

Making a day of it

This one is a day ride already, but you could always tag the **Claerwen Valley** loop (page 75) onto it if you really need more.

Making a weekend of it

The **Claerwen Valley** (page 75) is the obvious one, but the **Doethie Valley** route (page 59) and the **Irfon Forest** loop (page 63) are also within sensible reach. There's also some man-made trails at Coed Trallwm.

SUMPTUOUS SINGLETRACK NEAR THE THREE RIGGLES

13 Radnor Forest

17km

Introduction

The Radnor Forest isn't a real forest: well, not in the accepted sense of the word anyway. The name comes from the area's previous incarnation as a hunting ground for the royals. Ironically though, like most of the upland regions of mid Wales, it is now carpeted in plantations anyway, so the name still rings true. The high point of the region is a mountain-come-moor, known as the Great Rhos, which reaches a respectable 660m – higher than any of the Cwmdeuddwr Hills, for example. This route climbs to within a few paces of this summit making it one of the highest routes in the book.

The Ride

This route boasts the toughest opening in the book, with an almost continuous climb of over 400 vertical metres in little over 5km to get the ball rolling. But it's never technical, so is definitely all rideable, and it does get most of the hard work out of the way early on – always a good thing. Once up, there's a quagmire to negotiate – all part of the Welsh MTB experience – and from then on, it's a cracker – definitely worth the pain and effort. The highlights are shared evenly between the quite gobsmacking views from the hills – the surrounding valleys resemble bottomless chasms in places – and some wonderful, non-technical riding that takes you both up and down. The drop from the Great Rhos is simply delightful: grassy, hemmed in by old walls, and dotted with some wonderful, natural whoopee-doos that will catch out the unsuspecting. And the traverse of the Black Brook valley, close to the wonderfully named Three Riggles, is breathtaking in more ways than one. Then there's that final descent, which just goes on forever. Made all the more interesting by the ominous looking danger signs at the top...

Note: This is not a great ride for wet conditions – definitely save it for a dry period.

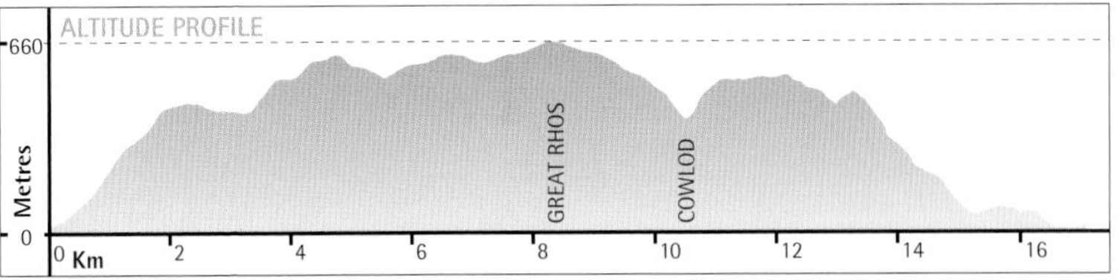

RADNOR FOREST **GRADE: ▲**

TOTAL DISTANCE: 17KM » **TOTAL ASCENT**: 700M » **TIME**: 2-3 HOURS » **START/FINISH**: NEW RADNOR, NEXT TO SCHOOL IN SCHOOL LANE » **START GRID REF**: SO 215607 » **SATNAV**: NEW RADNOR » **OS MAP**: EXPLORER 200; LANDRANGER 148
PUB: RADNOR ARMS, NEW RADNOR, TEL: 01544 350 232; THE FFOREST INN, ON THE A44, TEL: 01544 350 526
CAFE: OLD STATION CARAVAN PARK, NEW RADNOR, TEL: 01544 350 543

13 RADNOR FOREST

Directions – Radnor Forest

S Ride back out of School Lane and turn **R** and then **R** again onto Water Street. Follow this to the top and keep **SA** up Mutton Dingle. Follow this steeply for about 1km up to a fork at the edge of a forestry plantation and bear **L** onto a double track trail. After 100m pass through a gate and follow the now grassy trail around the forest, still climbing, and then keep **SA** to drop slightly to the head of Ystol Bach Valley.

2 Go through the gate and continue upwards and around to the right until the track runs out close to the edge of forestry. Keep **SA** for a few metres to the fence and locate a stile that allows access to the obvious forest track.

3 Turn **L** to climb on the forest trail and **ignore** fork to the left after 500m and then two to the right, to keep close to the edge of the forest until you reach a major junction by a fence corner. Bear **R** here (usually muddy) and follow this for 200m to a turning on the **L**. Take this and follow it out of the forest to a gate.

4 Go through the gate and keep **SA** with the fence to the right to a gate. Go through to continue with the fence now to the left. Drop to meet a broad track and turn **L** onto it, then immediately **L** again onto a faint, narrow grassy track that leads steeply uphill. Follow this up and through a gate and keep **SA** to loop around the head of a narrow valley. Now keep **SA** again through a gate, crossing a track then dropping into a deep valley (small pool to your right) on faint, easy-to-miss singletrack, where the path becomes much more obvious.

5 Climb out of this dip and follow the singletrack along the side of a spectacular valley. Keep **SA** onto a good track at the top and drop to a gate. Through this to drop with a fence (and a bomb sign!) to your left. Follow this down to a footbridge/ford at the very bottom.

6 Cross the river and turn **R** onto the track. Shortly after, fork **L** on a tarmac drive, through a blue gate. The track soon becomes dirt: stay with this as it contours around the hillside to a tarmac lane and drops to the B4372. Turn **L** here to return to the bottom of Mutton Dingle, and then retrace your earlier tracks back to the car park.

Great Rhos is a mixture of English and Welsh, with Rhos meaning Moorland. No prizes for guessing why the hill got its name.

Making a day of it

There are numerous rideable tracks and trails south of the A44, and these could easily be linked with the route and the town of New Radnor, where a pub lunch in the Radnor Arms could spice up the occasion.

Making a weekend of it

The nearest bundle would be the **Llanbedr Hill** loop (page 69) but neither of the **Elan Valley** loops (pages 75 and 81) or the **Irfon Forest** (page 63) are too far away. Nor is Coed Trallwm if you fancy a man-made trail.

GREAT SINGLETRACK ON Y GRUG

14 Foel Fadian – Machynlleth 24km

Introduction

North of the mighty Pumlumon, the mid Wales mountains start to taper away slightly, eventually dipping into the Dovey Valley close to the new age centre of Machynlleth, famous for it's Centre for Alternative Technology, and a fairly impressive clock tower. It's a scenic corner of Wales, with lofty rounded hills, steep-sided valleys and a few remote lakes dotted around too. The Glyndwr's Way National Trail crosses the hills above the town where he tried to install the first Welsh Parliament, and the River Severn rises up in these mountains too.

The Ride

This is an interesting sortie into an area that might not seem obvious. But a couple of the trails are as good as anything in the book, making it well worth the effort of getting off the beaten track a bit. The first of these comes early and is quite unexpected as you cruise across the sheep pasture that leads to it. A tumbledown wall top provides an innocuous opening, but this quickly morphs into a section of superb serpentine singletrack that sweeps across the steep hillside before plunging awkwardly to a remote stream crossing. The second big descent is perhaps a little more obvious as it plummets steeply from the ride's highpoint close to the summit of Foel Fadian. But it would be difficult to predict the quality, especially the tricky little slabby section, which will definitely test tyre traction. The rest of the descent's fun too, but it does lead to a brutal climb of almost 400m, so keep something in reserve.

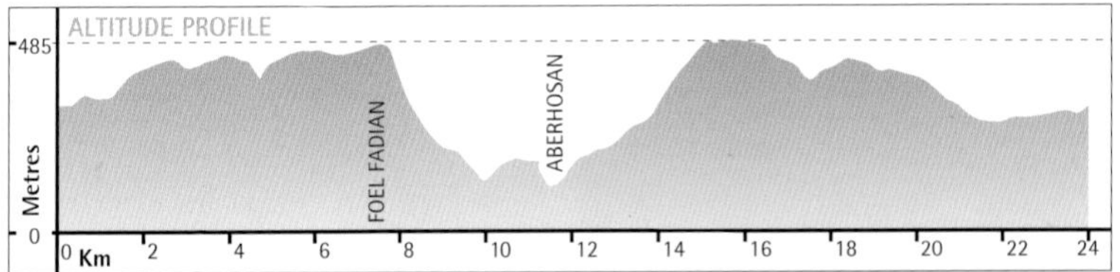

FOEL FADIAN – MACHYNLLETH **GRADE: ▲**

TOTAL DISTANCE: 24KM » **TOTAL ASCENT**: 890M » **TIME**: 2.5–4 HOURS » **START/FINISH**: BETWEEN STAYLITTLE AND DYLIFE
START GRID REF: SN 873939 » **SATNAV**: DYLIFE (NEAREST) » **OS MAP**: EXPLORER 215; LANDRANGER
PUB: THE STAR, DYLIFE, TEL: 01650 521 345 » **CAFÉ**: NONE

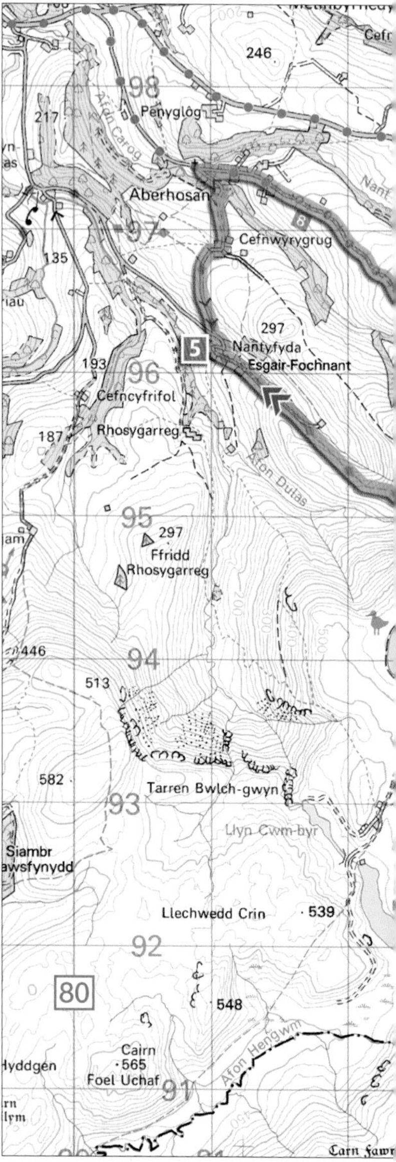

246
98
Penyglôg
217
Afon Carog
Aberhosan
8
97
Cefnwyrygrug
135
297
5
Nantyfyda
Esgair-Fochnant
193
96
Cefncyfrifol
Rhosygarreg
187
Afon Dulas
95
297
Ffridd
Rhosygarreg
446
94
513
582
Tarren Bwlch-gwyn
93
Llyn Cwm-byr
Siambr
Llechwedd Crin
539
92
80
548
Cairn
565
Foel Uchaf
91
Afon Hengwm

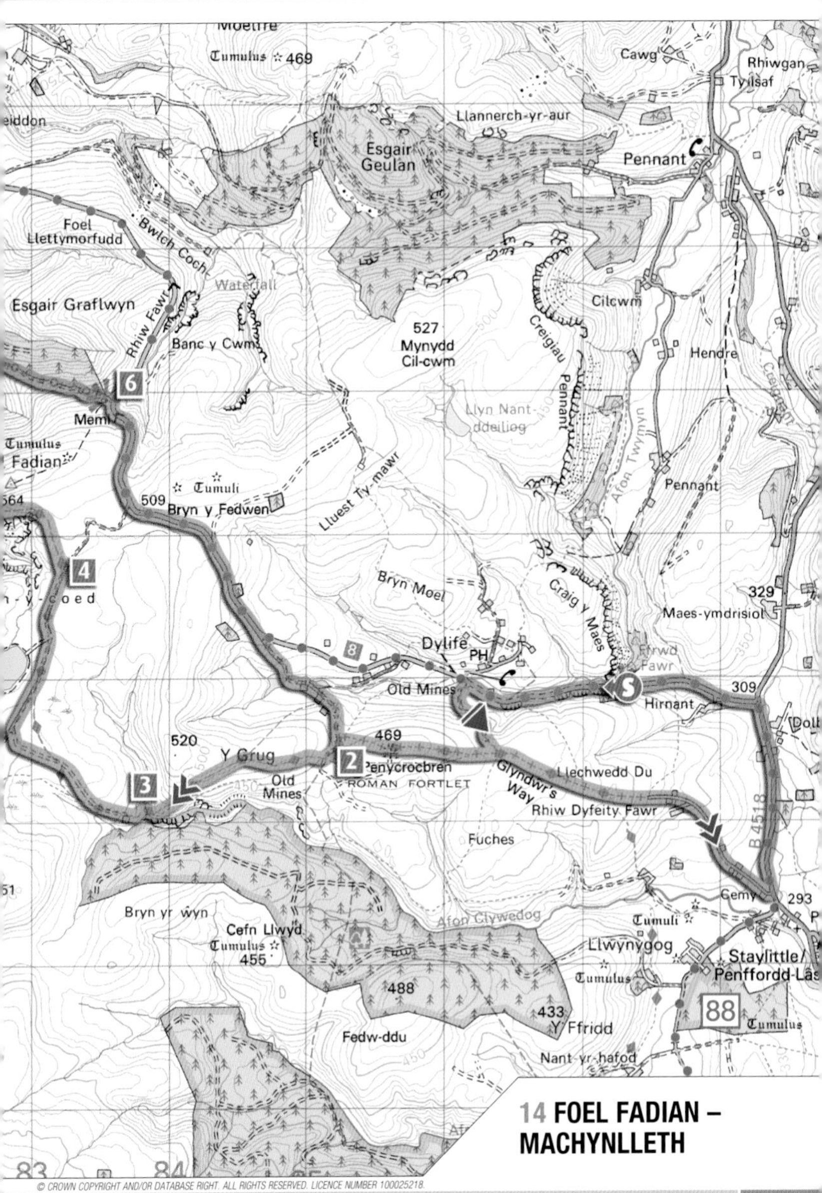

14 FOEL FADIAN – MACHYNLLETH

Directions – Foel Fadian – Machynlleth

S Turn **R** out of the car park and climb on tarmac for 1.5km to a gravel track on the **L** (opposite the Star pub). Climb steeply up to a tall fingerpost on the ridge top and turn **R** onto the main track to follow it over Penycrocbren and down to a boggy junction with another gravel track.

2 Turn **L** for 200m to bridleway on the **R**. Take this and follow the line of the grass covered wall (the best riding's actually on the top of the wall). This turns into singletrack and plummets steeply down to a bridge.

3 Climb the opposite bank and keep **R** of a sheep pen to join a good track. Follow this for 200m and turn **L** onto a waymarked bridleway. This swings back right to join the main track and continues past Glaslyn to a waymarked turning on the **L**.

4 This climbs slightly then drops steeply down the side of Foel Fadian. Keep **L** at a fork, and follow the sunken track down to a gate. Now keep **SA** to farm buildings at Esgair Fochnant, and continue to Nantyfyda, where you bear **sharp R** to join the road.

5 Turn **R** at a fork, and follow the road all the way into Aberhosan, where you turn sharp **R** to ride up through the hamlet. Keep **SA** to climb the 'No Through Road' to Ty Gwyn, and then climb **SA** for nearly 3km to another road by the Wynford Vaughan Thomas memorial.

6 Turn **R** to the brow and drop to a gated track on the **R**. Drop beneath houses and climb back onto the ridge, where you revisit the junction you visited earlier. Bear **L** to retrace your outward tracks for just over 1km and then keep **SA** to drop to farm buildings. Keep **SA** on the road and turn **L** at the bottom, and **L** again to finish.

At 510m, the part of the trail that runs across the flank of Foel Fadian is the highest point of the Glyndwr's Way National Trail.

Making a weekend of it

The best bet is the Nant yr Arian trail centre – some of the most enjoyable trails in the country – or the Machynlleth trails, including the excellent Cli-Machx just north of the town.

SECTION 3

North Wales
and the Snowdonia National Park

The highest mountain in Wales provides the biggest climb and descent in the book, but there's so much more to North Wales than this. Snowdonia provides mountain biking in real mountains but don't overlook the outlying ranges of the Berwyns and Clwyds, there's plenty to go at there too...

DESCENDING TO LLANBERIS (ROUTE 18) PHOTO: JOHN COEFIELD

THE AUTHOR DESCENDING THE SNOWDON RANGER PATH (ROUTE 18) PHOTO: JOHN COEFIELD

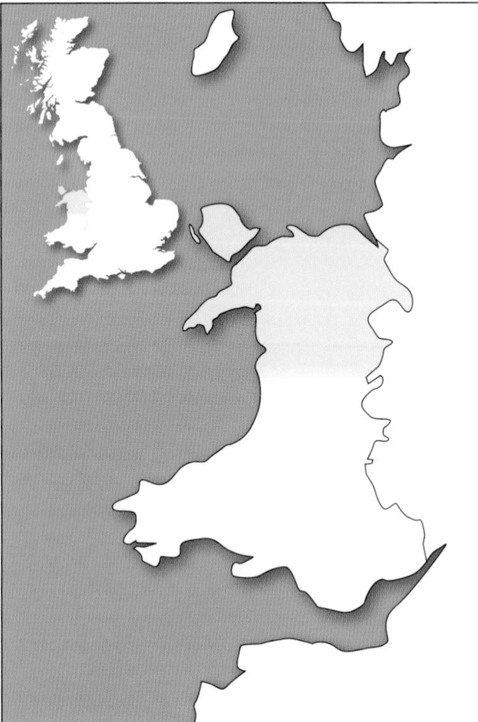

North Wales & the Snowdonia National Park
route finder

Holyhead

NORTH WALES AND THE SNOWDONIA NATIONAL PARK

FINE SINGLETRACK ABOVE KINGS YHA

15 The Foothills of Cadair – Cadair Idris 44km

Introduction

Cadair Idris is southern Snowdonia's Snowdon in terms of reputation and popularity. And despite the fact it has no train to the top, or no café to revive tired summiteers, it still sees thousands of visitors every year. The mountain towers over the small town of Dolgellau, on the banks of the stunning Mawddach Estuary. And it offers superb views in all directions, sometimes as far as Snowdon in the north, and Pen y Fan in the Brecon Beacons, to the south. The western tip of the ridge it sits upon dips its toes in the sea a short distance south of Barmouth; and the eastern end nudges up against the spectacular Dovey Hills.

The Ride

There is a bridleway to the summit of Cadair, but the out and back nature of the route tends to make it a less sought after tick than Snowdon.

It's perhaps better then to make the most of the spider's web of tracks and trails on the mountain's northern and western foothills, and instead engineer a long but relatively straightforward loop around these. It's basically a two up, two down; the opening section hurdling the western edge of the ridge, before dropping steeply back to sea level in the seaside town of Llwyngwril; and the homeward leg clambering up over the 300m contour line before plummeting back down to the valley floor in two stages. The first of these is fast and furious on well-surfaced tracks that don't throw up too many surprises; the second is a very different kettle of fish that offers some much tougher going, especially the climb from the Youth Hostel. All in, it's a softer touch than most of the North Wales routes in this book. But at 44km it's still quite a challenge.

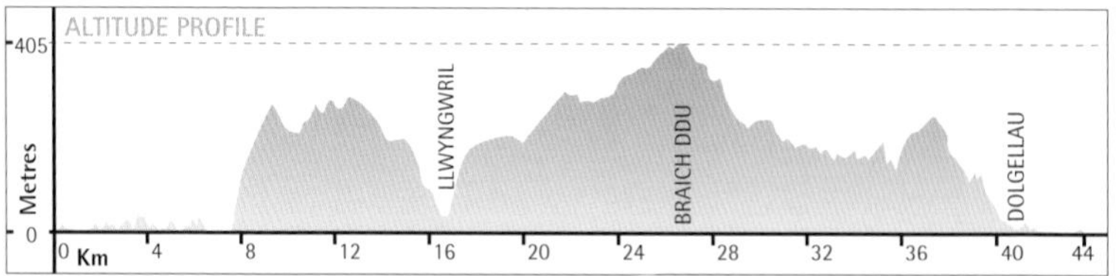

THE FOOTHILLS OF CADAIR – CADAIR IDRIS **GRADE: ▲**

TOTAL DISTANCE: 44KM » **TOTAL ASCENT**: 1,380M » **TIME**: 5–6 HOURS » **START/FINISH**: PENMAENPOOL, DOLGELLAU
START GRID REF: SH 695185 » **SATNAV**: PENMAENPOOL » **OS MAP**: EXPLORER OL23; LANDRANGER 124
PUB: GEORGE III AT THE START; GWERNAN HOTEL, SHORT DETOUR NEAR THE END TEL: 01341 422 488 » **CAFÉ**: NONE ON ROUTE

CONTINUES ON PAGE 108

15 THE FOOTHILLS OF CADAIR – CADAIR IDRIS – PART 1

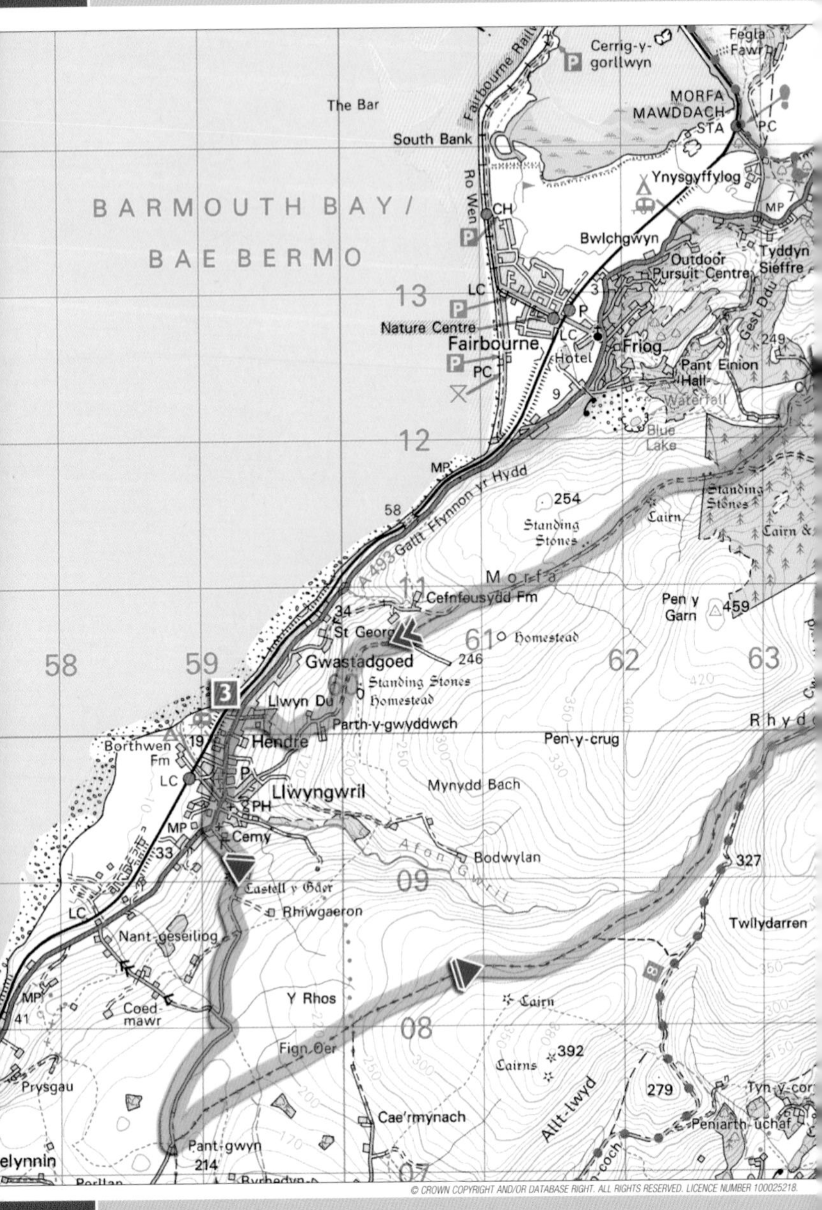

BARMOUTH BAY /
BAE BERMO
Fairbourne Railway
Cerrig-y-gorllwyn
Fegla Fawr
The Bar
MORFA MAWDDACH STA
PC
South Bank
Ro Wen
Ynysgyffylog
CH
MP
Bwlchgwyn
Outdoor Pursuit Centre
Tyddyn Sieffre
13
LC
P
Nature Centre
Fairbourne
LC
Hotel
Friog
Gest Ddu
249
Pant Einion Hall
PC
9
Waterfall
Blue Lake
12
MP
A 493 Gallt Ffynnon yr Hydd
254
Standing Stones
Cairn
58
Standing Stones
Cairn &
Morfa
11
Cefnfeusydd Fm
34
St George
Pen y Garn
459
61
Homestead
246
58
59
Gwastadgoed
62
63
3
Standing Stones
Homestead
Llwyn Du
Parth-y-gwyddwch
Rhyd
Borthwen Fm
19
Hendre
Pen-y-crug
LC
P
Llwyngwril
Mynydd Bach
PH
MP
Cemy
33
Afon Gwril
Bodwylan
327
Castell y Gaer
09
Rhiwgaeron
LC
Nant-geseiliog
Twllydarren
8
MP
41
Y Rhos
Cairn
Coed-mawr
08
Fign Oer
392
Cairns
Prysgau
Allt-lwyd
279
Tyn-y-cornel
Cae'rmynach
Peniarth-uchaf
Pant-gwyn
214
elynnin
Perllan
Byrhedyn
07

CONTINUES ON PAGE 107

15 THE FOOTHILLS OF CADAIR – CADAIR IDRIS – PART 2

Directions – The Foothills of Cadair – Cadair Idris

S Join the well-surfaced Mawddach Trail at the back of the car park and follow it easily downstream for 7.5km to a small road at an inlet near Arthog (don't go as far as the main bridge). Turn **L** onto the road and ride up to the A493, where you turn **R** and then immediately **L** onto a very steep climb.

2 Stay on this for 2km to a crossroads and bear **R** onto a tarmac track. Follow this for 4km and then, as it drops to the right, keep **SA** onto a grassy track that traverses the hillside before eventually dropping steeply to the roadhead above Llwyngwril. Turn **R** on to a waymarked, walled bridleway and follow this down through a copse and through a gate to join a drive that leads to the main road.

3 Turn **L** to head through the village and then turn **L** by a large Celtic cross. Climb steeply to a T-junction and turn **L** to continue to a track junction by a derelict building. Turn **sharp L** onto a grassy track and follow this for 4km, where you merge into another track above the Afon Dyffryn. Continue **SA** to the edge of a forest and **ignore** tracks on the right to drop to a junction. Keep **R** to drop to the road.

4 Turn **R** and stay with it for 4km to the large Cadair Idris car park at Ty-nant. Turn **L** onto a bridleway that runs alongside the car park and follow this past farm buildings and down a field edge to a gate above a steep section. Drop down to the **L** and through a gap in the wall and then continue down on a good track. Look for a waymark sending you **R**, off the main track (**easy to miss**), and drop to cross the stream.

5 Follow the singletrack up out of the wood to a gate. Keep **L** to drop down the next field edge to an obvious rocky ramp on the **R**. (If you reach the buildings, you've gone too far.)

6 Take this and keep left of the wall to a gate by a barn. Keep ahead, climbing between walls to a gate that leads onto open ground. Follow the obvious track down and keep **L** at a fork to drop alongside the wall to buildings and the road at the bottom. Turn **R** onto the road and then **L** onto the main road.

7 Drop into Dolgellau and turn **sharp L** at the end of the road. Follow this to the A483 and turn **R**, over the bridge, then **L** onto the cycleway. Follow this back to the car park.

Cadair Idris translates to the 'Chair of Idris,' but exactly who Idris was, is less certain, with some believing he was a giant and others, a warrior.

Optional Route – tackling the Summit (16km/800m ascent)

OR Start at Llanfihangel-y-pennant (SH 672089) and follow the lane first north-east and then north until it turns into a dirt track and climbs steeply to Hafotty Gwastadfryn. The dirt gives way to a grassy trail that then turns to a paved path and climbs all the way to the summit. The descent is the reverse.

Making a day of it

It's quite long already, but there's no stopping anyone hopping over the toll bridge from Penmaenpool and then linking up with the eastern corner of the **Pont-Scethin** loop (page 113) to turn it into a true marathon.

Making a weekend of it

The **Pont-Scethin** loop (page 113) starts just a few miles up the road, if you want to keep it natural. Alternatively, there's Coed y Brenin within easy reach, and the Cli-machx Trail at Corris starts just a few miles south of the mountain.

GREAT VIEWS BACK OVER BARMOUTH AND THE SEA

CROSSING PONT-SCETHIN

16 **Pont-Scethin** – Rhinogau

19km

Introduction

The Rhinogs, or Rhinogau to give them their proper name, are the jagged, almost shark-tooth mountains that tower over the forestry of Coed y Brenin (to the west if you've never noticed). Although they aren't particularly high, they are notorious for being some of Snowdonia's toughest and most rugged peaks, with few paths, plenty of rock and almost impenetrable heather in places. Fortunately though, it's the northern end of the range that earns this reputation, and the hills to the south, between Barmouth and the forest, are considerably friendlier, even if they are slightly taller. Pont-Scethin is a picturesque old packhorse bridge that spans the Afon Ysgethin, a mountain stream that issues straight from the heart of these southern hills. It forms the centrepiece of one of North Wales's best rides.

The Ride

This is quite a short outing but it's also a tough one, and there won't be many on the hunt for a few extra kilometres come the end. It starts with a good long road climb from the A496 – the perfect way to get the muscles warmed up – and then gravel takes over before a short, sweet bonus descent down to the bridge. The climb from here is gruesome, even with the help of flagstones to take the worst out of the wet ground. And by the time you make the top, you'll be wondering what you are doing here. It'll all be alright in a minute, with a wonderful descent down the narrow ridge of Braich, followed by a long traverse, with wonderful views south to Cadair Idris. The climb to Bwlch y Rhiwgyr isn't quite as brutal as the previous one and it's downhill all the way from here. The descent starts rough, but soon smoothes a little into a full-pelt blast back to the banks of the Ysgethin, where a fun forest descent leads back to the car park.

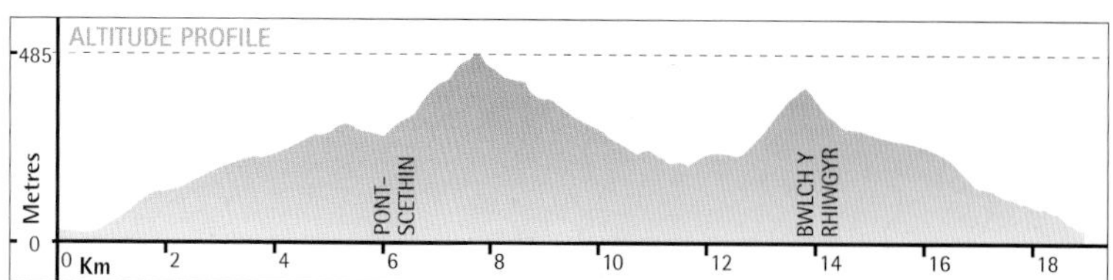

PONT-SCETHIN – RHINOGAU **GRADE: ▲**

TOTAL DISTANCE: 19KM » **TOTAL ASCENT**: 850M » **TIME**: 3-4 HOURS » **START/FINISH**: TAL-Y-BONT
START GRID REF: SH 589218 » **SATNAV**: LL43 2AN » **OS MAP**: EXPLORER OL18; LANDRANGER 124
PUB: THE YSGETHIN INN, TEL: 01341 247 578 » **CAFÉ**: BARMOUTH

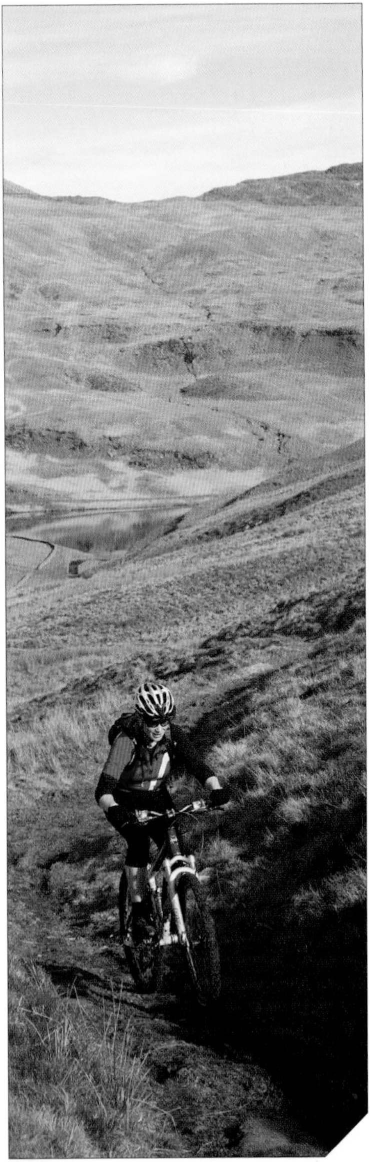

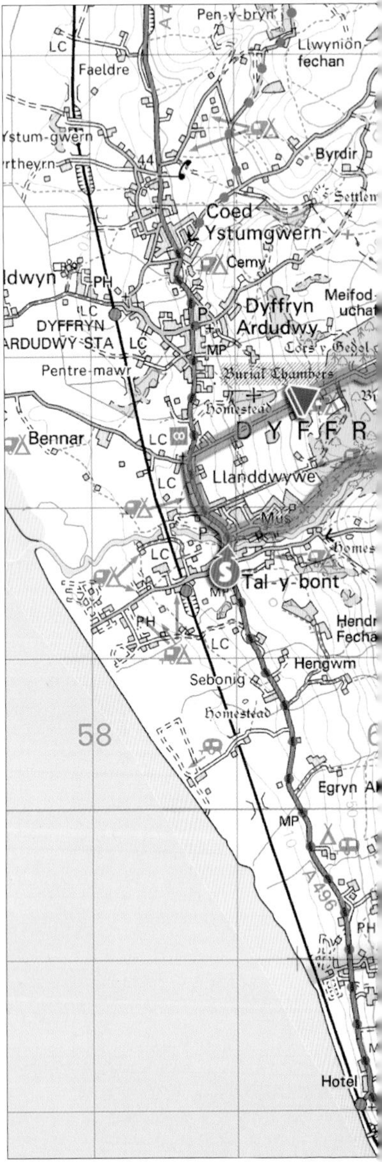

Pen-y-bryn
Llwyniön-fechan
LC
Faeldre
Ystum-gwern
44
Byrdir
Coed Ystumgwern
Cemy
PH
Meifod uchaf
Dyffryn Ardudwy
DYFFRYN ARDUDWY STA
LC
P
MP
Cors y Gedol
Pentre-mawr
Burial Chambers
Homestead
Bennar
D Y F F R
Llanddwywe
Mus
Tal-y-bont
Hengwm
Sebonig
Homestead
58
Egryn
MP
A 496
PH
Hotel

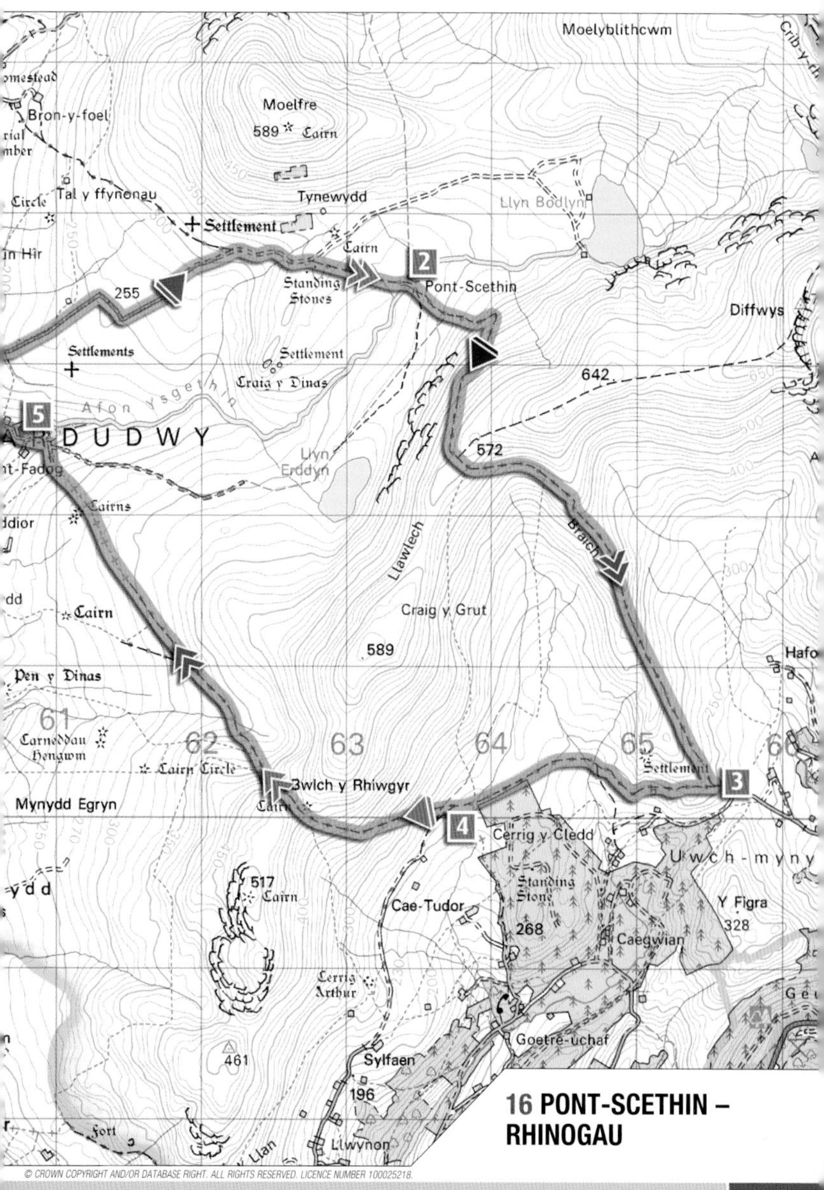

16 PONT-SCETHIN – RHINOGAU

Directions – Pont-Scethin – Rhinogau

S Turn **R** onto the road and continue for 500m to a narrow lane on the **R**. Climb this steeply for 1.5km to a junction and turn **R** onto a road that soon becomes dirt. Keep **R** at a track junction and then, after another 500m, look carefully for a faint track that forks **R** where the track swings left. Follow this down to Pont-Scethin.

2 Cross the bridge and climb over boggy ground keeping to the **L** track. This leads to a right-hand hairpin bend and a very tough climb. Continue to the top and a cairn and go through a gate before keeping **L** to traverse the hillside. Go through another gate and turn **R** to follow the wall down through a succession of gates. When the field narrows, follow a walled track down to its end at Banc y Fran.

3 Go through a gate and look for a faint track that comes in from the **R** (if you get to the road then you've gone too far!). Follow this around the hillside and through a number of gates. Continue until it becomes gravel and leads to a junction of tracks.

4 Turn **R** and then, after 100m, **L** onto a narrow track that climbs steeply between rocky outcrops. Go through the gate at the very top and descend to another. Now follow the obvious track down through fields to a wall above the river. Follow the wall to the river at Pont Farchog.

5 From the bridge, climb for 200m and then turn **L** onto a waymarked bridleway. Follow this down through the woods to the riverbank and continue to a fork after 1km. Keep **R** at the fork (not down the steps) and then, after another 50m, fork **L**. Continue into Tal-y-bont and bear **L** to return to the car park.

i No surprises for those with good French or Latin, '**pont**' means '**bridge**' in Welsh.

Making a day of it

It could be joined with the **Cadair Idris** loop (page 105) to make a real epic.

Making a weekend of it

For lovers of the natural stuff, there's the **Cadair Idris** loop (page 105), which starts on the other side of the Mawddach. Or if you fancy some singletrack action, head straight to Coed y Brenin without passing go or collecting £200...

THE TOP OF THE FIRST BIG CLIMB

SLATEY SINGLETRACK NEAR LLANGYNOG

17 Berwyn Hills

50km

Introduction

The Berwyn Hills represent the forgotten side of North Wales, with most of the attention being heaped on either the holiday centres of the north coast or Snowdonia National Park. Yet they have much going for them, including easy access from the Midlands and north-west England, and also some great scenery, including Cadair Berwyn – the highest mountain in Wales outside of the National Parks. The Pistyll Rhaeadr waterfalls bring in a fair few visitors to the area though, as does the recent black grouse reintroduction program, which has helped reverse a serious decline in numbers of these wonderful dancing birds.

The Ride

This is a true epic; definitely worth saving for a good day so the riding can be savoured as the hilltops are wild, exposed and not a place to be in foul weather. It's a three up, three down outing, with three very different climbs; the first on tarmac, the second on good rough tracks, and the third on a variety of surfaces. And for the effort expended, there are some fine descents; a mixed bag from the grouse moors to the woodland near Pennant, a rocky horror show from the touching Wayfarer Memorial to Llanarmon Dyffryn Ceiriog, and the last from the flanks of Glan-hafon all the way down to the finish at Llangynog. This one starts scarily steep on a rough, grassy singletrack that tests nerve and brakes alike. It eases temporarily as it picks up a farm drive, but soon leaves this to give a perfect grand finale of scintillating singletrack that darts across the hillside and skips over the slatey remains of one of the area's many quarries. *This descent can also be enjoyed on a shorter outing by following tarmac out from Llangynog to Penbontfawr and then climbing up to meet the final climb above Llanrhaeadr-ym-Mochnant.*

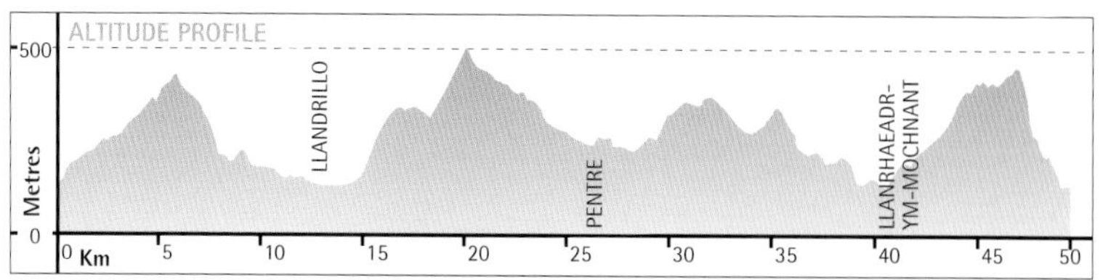

BERWYN HILLS **GRADE: ▲**

TOTAL DISTANCE: 50KM » **TOTAL ASCENT**: 1,750M » **TIME**: 5–7 HOURS » **START/FINISH**: LLANGYNOG
START GRID REF: SJ 053261 » **SATNAV**: SY10 0EX » **OS MAP**: EXPLORER 255; LANDRANGER 125
PUB: THE WEST ARMS HOTEL, LLANARMON DYFFRYN CEIRIOG, TEL: 01691 600 665 » **CAFÉ**: NONE

CONTINUES ON PAGE 122
Pennant
Foel Fawr
Craig Berwyn
Cadair Berwyn
Moel yr Ewig
Moel Sych
Llyn Lluncaws
Esgeiriau
Y Berwyn National Nature Reserve
Cerrig Duon
Milltir Gerrig
Blaen Glaswen
Stone Circle
Stone Row
Afon Disgynfa
Pistyll Rhaeadr
Tan-y-pistyll
Post Gwyn
Tre-rhiwarth
Blaen-rhiwarth
Cwm Rhiwarth
Tyn-y-ffynonydd
Hafod Hir
Craig Blaen-rhiwarth
Bryn Mawr
Y Clogydd
Craig Boeth
Ty-mawr
Llwyn-onn
Bedd Crynddyn
Tre-y-llan
Yr Eithin
Craig y Castell
Craig Pen-y-buarth
Pencraig
Fort
Craig Rhiwarth
Aber Cysgod
Pennant Melangell
Cwm Pennant
Llangynog
Llechwedd-y-garth
Cave
Tai uchaf
Ochr-glan-hafon
Llwyn Onn
Glan-hafon
Y Gar
Pentre
Glanhafon
Bryndre
Moel Dimoel
Rhyd-y-felin
Pengwern
Cyrniau
Pwlliago
Llwyn-onn
Tap y Gigfran
Cwm Llech
Craig-Las
Cwm Dwygo
Pistyll y Gyfyng
Pen y Craig-Las
Bwlch y Main
Cwmwr Uchaf
Peniarth
Wern

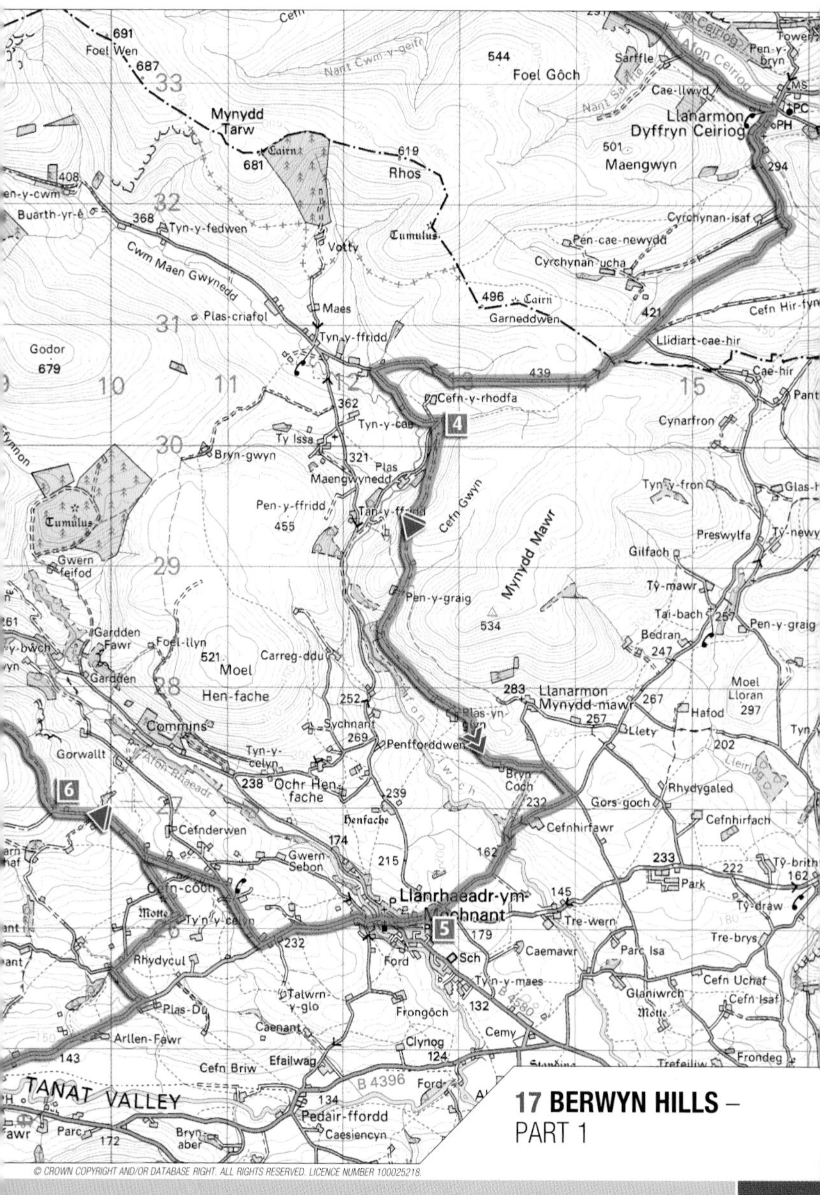

17 BERWYN HILLS – PART 1

Llandrillo
Cadwst
Pennant
Tyfos
Hendwr
Hendre
Coed y Glyn
Blaen-y-glyn
Rhos-y-maerdy
Moel yr Henfaes
Coedydd Branas
Branas isaf
Tyn-y-ddol
Ty-uchaf
Tyn-y-wern
Moel-is-y-goedwig
Cilan
Pont Cilan
Llawr Cilan
Tre'r-llan
Llechwedd Cilan
Llechwedd
Tyn-y-coed
Garthian
Pentre
Plas-yn-Dinam
Blaen-y-dre
Cefn-Pen-llety
Blaen Dinam
Nurse Gron
Cefn Penagored
Cwm Pennant
Settlement
Trawsnant
Clochnant
Ring Cairn
Carnedd y Ci
Moel Pearce
Hen Dŵr
Nant y Cyllyll
Ffynnon Maen Milgi
Cadair Bronwen
Bwlch Maen Gwynedd
Pant-y-llyn
Afon Dinam
Cefn Llystyn
Rhyd-y-Gethin
Afon Ceidiog
Yr Aran
Cairns
Blaen-y-cwm
Yr Oron
Nant Crechwyl
Nant Cwm Tywyll
Nant Esgeiriau
Pennant
Nant y Waun
Cwm-pen-llydan
Esgeiriau
Foel Fawr
Craig Berwyn
Cadair Berwyn
Moel yr Ewig
Moel Sych
Llyn Lluncaws
Y Berwyn National Nature Reserve
Cawnant Coch
Cerrig Duon
Cwm yr Eithin
Cwm-Rhiwiau
Stone Circle
Stone Row
Blaen Glaswen
Afon Disgynfa
Milltir Gerrig
Craig Wen
Waterfall
Pistyll
Nant y Llyn
B E R W Y N

CONTINUES ON PAGE 121

17 BERWYN HILLS – PART 2

Directions – Berwyn Hills

S Turn **R** out of the car park and follow the B4391 out of the village and up above the Tannat Valley. Continue for 6km to a track on the **R** at the very top. Follow this for 200m, and then bear **L** onto a rough track that you follow for 2km to Blaen-y-cwm. Keep **SA**, onto the road for another 5km to Llandrillo.

2 Turn **R** to ride through the village and keep **SA** for 2km to a turning on the **R** by a telephone box. Climb past Ty'n-y-parc and keep **SA** to a crossroads; bear **L** here to continue to climb for another 4km to the Wayfarer Memorial plaque at the top.

3 Keep **SA** to descend for 4km to the road, and keep **SA** again to continue to a crossroads in Llanarmon Dyffryn Ceiriog. Turn **R** and follow the road for over 4km to a T-junction at the bottom of a hill. Turn **L** (signed *Llanrhaeadr*) and then, on a sharp right-hand bend, bear **L** onto a track.

4 Climb for 1km, and then cruise easily around the hillside before dropping to a road head. Keep **SA** to a T-junction and turn **R** for 300m, then **R** again. Now drop to the B4580 and turn **R** onto this. Continue into Llanrhaeadr-ym-Mochnant and keep **SA** (turning off the B4580) to climb out the other side.

5 Continue for 2km, to where it levels, and turn **R** into a narrow lane that leads past a telephone box to a fork, where you keep **L**. Now keep **SA** for nearly 2km, until you reach a barn at the head of the lane.

6 Bear **R** and follow the track for 3km to a boggy section by a gate. Keep **SA** for another 300m (very boggy) and then bear **L**, through a gate. Keep ahead passing a waymarker that marks the start of the descent.

7 Descend steeply, around switchbacks, to the bottom, but **don't** get drawn into the bottom left corner. Aim 100m right of this, where a gate leads onto a good track. Follow this for 500m to a fork at a gate, and bear **R** to drop down to a stream.

8 Cross the stream and bear **L** on the far bank, and follow this up to join a broad track, where you turn **L**. Go through a gate and fork **R** onto singletrack. Keep **SA** through a wood and down over an old slate quarry to the road at the bottom. Bear **R** to return to Llangynog.

Optional Route – Short Loop

OR Turn **R** out of the car park and then take the first turning on the **R**, turning **R** almost immediately again to follow a narrow lane out of the village. Keep **SA** for nearly 5km, to a T-junction above Penybontfawr. Turn **L** to climb steadily for 2km and bear **L** onto another narrow lane, with a cottage on the corner. Bear **R** after 300m and then, as the road swings left, keep **SA** onto a track. Follow this through a farmyard to a crossroads, where you keep **SA**. Continue to a junction with a road and bear **L** to climb towards the road head at a barn. Follow the directions opposite from point **6**.

Llanrhaeadr-ym-Mochnant translates roughly as **'Village of the waterfall on the pig stream.'**

Making a weekend of it

Head north for the **Clwydian Hills** (page 139) or west for the Snowdonia routes. Another alternative is the trail centre at Coed Llandegla.

DESCENDING THE RANGER PATH ***PHOTO:*** *JOHN COEFIELD*

18 Snowdon

21km

Introduction

Snowdon isn't just the highest mountain in Wales. At 1,085m, it also towers above anything in the Lake District, making it way taller than anything else south of the Scottish border. But there's more to Snowdon (or Yr Wyddfa, as it's known in Welsh) than pure height. It's actually a stunning mountain; tall and proud with shapely ridges and a rugged, rocky pyramid of a summit. And it somehow manages to maintain an air of grandeur and dignity despite the attentions of thousands of train riding tourists that batter its upper reaches throughout the summer. Ride it when it's quiet or out of season to really get the best out of it.

NOTE: *There is a voluntary restriction on cycling on the Snowdon bridleways between 10am and 5pm from 1st May until 30th September. Please adhere to this to ensure continued access.*

WARNING: *This is a very rocky ride, with some serious drainage gullies. Take plenty of heavy duty tubes with you.*

The Ride

Riding Snowdon could be seen as a rite of passage for budding Welsh MTBers, not to mention a cool thing to tell your mates. But it's so much more than that, and this route is one of the best routes in this book, as well as one of the toughest. The ride options are threefold: up and down by the Llanberis Path – the quickest and most rideable of the up-and-down routes (the Ranger Path involves far more pushing); up the Llanberis Path and down the Ranger Path – the best of both worlds but two cars are needed; or the full circuit from the Ranger Station over Bwlch Maesgwm to Llanberis before climbing the Llanberis Path and descending the Ranger Path. This is by far the toughest choice, and the way we've described here, but the sinuous singletrack descent from Bwlch Maesgwm to Llanberis makes the extra effort worthwhile, and the final drop down the Ranger Path is the only real way to end a ride on Wales's highest mountain. Don't think of this loop as just a ride; think of it as an event!

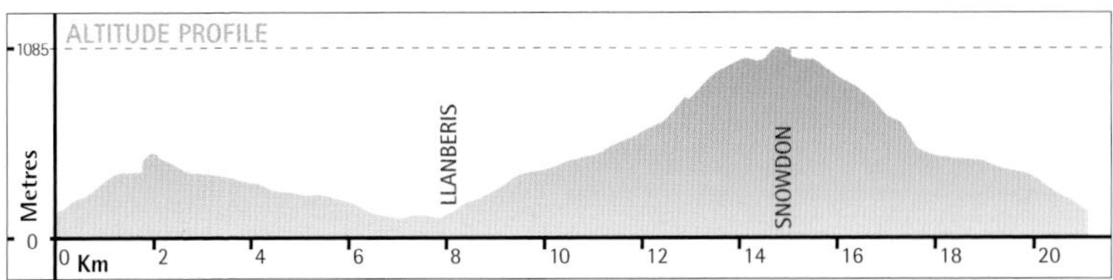

SNOWDON **GRADE: ▲**

TOTAL DISTANCE: 21KM » **TOTAL ASCENT**: 1,430M » **TIME**: 4–6 HOURS » **START/FINISH**: SNOWDON RANGER STATION
START GRID REF: SH 563551 » **SATNAV**: RHYD-DDU » **OS MAP**: EXPLORER OL17; LANDRANGER 115
PUB: THE HEIGHTS HOTEL, LLANBERIS, TEL: 01286 238 235 » **CAFÉ**: PETE'S EATS, LLANBERIS, TEL: 01286 870 117; PENCEUNANT ISAF TEAROOM (ON THE CLIMB FROM LLANBERIS), TEL: 01286 872 606

EASY CLIMBING LOW DOWN ON THE RANGER PATH PHOTO: JOHN COEFIELD

Llanberis
GILFACH DDU STA
Museum
Wks
Dolbadarn Castle (rems of)
Power Station
Llyn Peris
Hotel
Coed Victoria
Waterfall
Wern
Fron
Burnt Mound
Ceunant Bach
403
Derlwyn
HEBRON STA
Nant Peris (Old Llanberis)
Ffynnon Peris
Gwastad
Brithdir
Adwyrwaen
Llyn Dwythwch
Tynyraelgerth
Hadodty Newydd
409
Cwm Dwythwch
Afon Arddu
Helfa
HALFWAY STA
Snowdon Mountain Railway
Halfway House
718
Llechog
Foel Gron
Foel Goch
605
Moel Cynghorion
674
CLOGWYN STA
Maen-du'r Arddu
467
Cwm Brwynog
Snowdon Ranger Path
Llyn Du'r Arddu
Llyn Ffynnon-y-gwas
Clogwyn Du'r Arddu
Garnedd Ugain
1065
Snowdon Ranger
Cwm Clogwyn
Bron-y-fedw
Llyn Coch
143
Afon Treweunydd
Llyn Nadroedd
SUMMIT STA
SNOWDON / YR WYDDFA
Afon Gwyrfai
Llyn y Dywarchen
238

18 SNOWDON

Directions – Snowdon

S Turn **L** out of the car park and almost immediately turn **R** onto a gravel drive that crosses the Welsh Highland Railway and continues up to a farm. Keep the house to your right and ride past it before bearing **R** through a gate (*Path* painted on rock ahead). Follow the path up around a series of switchbacks and over a short technical section to a junction marked by a small post on the left (**easy to miss**).

2 Turn **L** and push steeply straight uphill (**G.O.A.P.**) on a vague path and continue until it eventually levels in a pass known as Bwlch Maesgwm. Keep ahead and go through a gate next to a stile in an obvious saddle.

3 Join a wonderful singletrack and stay with it all the way until it eventually broadens and levels. Continue to a junction with a turning on the right and a gate straight ahead. Turn **R** to pass in front of a house and drop down the road, through a farmyard, to the High Street in Llanberis.

4 Turn **R** and then first **R**, next to a car workshop, to follow the narrow lane past a church and around to the left. Ignore a footpath to the right (signed *Waterfalls*) and drop beneath the railway line to a T-junction. Turn **R** here and climb steeply up the lane for 800m to a gate on the **L** (signed *Snowdon*). Take this and now follow the Llanberis Path upwards, all the way to the summit (some sections **G.O.A.P.**).

5 To return by the Ranger Path, retrace the last part of the climb from the summit for approximately 600m to the broad, level area where the path from Carnedd Ugain merges and then cross the railway line to locate a clear stony track that starts running parallel to it and then veers away slightly. Follow this down over a shoulder and down a series of zigzags (steep in places, a couple of carries likely needed). Continue all the way down until you rejoin the outward leg near point **2** and then retrace your tyre tracks back to the car park.

Out and back option

OR Start in Llanberis and make your way to the Mountain Railway Station. Continue south along the main road for 100m and then take the first turning on the **R**. Follow this for 1km to a gate on the **L** (signed *Snowdon*). Follow the Llanberis Path upwards, all the way to the summit. Return via the same route.

A–B option (Llanberis to Ranger Station)

Follow the Out and Back option to the summit, then follow the route description from point **5**.

NOTE: *There is a voluntary restriction on cycling on the Snowdon bridleways between 10am and 5pm from 1st May until 30th September. Please adhere to this to ensure continued access.*

WARNING: *This is a very rocky ride, with some serious drainage gullies. Take plenty of heavy duty tubes with you.*

Snowdon is called **Yr Wyddfa** (loosely pronounced **Er With-va**) in Welsh.

Making a weekend of it

The **Carneddau** loop (page 133) is only a couple of valleys over and would make an excellent weekend of natural riding. Alternatively, you're not far from the Marin Trail at Gwydyr Forest or the singletrack trails at Penmachno.

THE HIGHEST POINT IN ENGLAND & WALES PHOTO: JOHN COEFIELD

SPECTACULAR FLAGSTONE BRIDGE ABOVE THE OGWEN VALLEY

19 The Carneddau – Snowdonia 27km

Introduction

The Carneddau is the northernmost mountain range in Snowdonia, but despite covering more square kilometres than both the Glyderau and the Snowdon ranges put together, and comprising of more high ground than either, it sees far fewer visitors, making it feel a lot wilder. The main Carneddau peaks run north-south forming a spine in the centre of the range, but this is no territory for mountain bikes. The easternmost hills, however, are penetrated by a pair of excellent trails that form the mainframe of this route.

The Ride

This is one of the toughest and most technical routes in the book, and is best suited to good, fit, technical riders, that are happy wrestling with the many challenges the high mountain environment throws at them. It offers top-notch riding in wonderfully remote places and is about as far removed from the trail centre experience as you could possibly get. In places it feels more like the Scottish Highlands than North Wales: a wonderfully satisfying outing for the capable and prepared. The highlight is the drop down the side of the remote Llyn Cowlyd: kilometres of serpentine singletrack – technical in places, sweet and easy rolling in others. The grand finale from the pass down to Capel Curig is wonderful too – a rocky horror show that's just about totally cleanable if you keep your momentum up. The climbs are steep but on tarmac, and there's an incredible steep descent on tarmac too – sorry, unavoidable to keep the circuit together. *A final word of warning: the section from the A5 up to Llyn Cowlyd is vague in places, boggy in others, and there are a few spots where the right of way is blocked altogether by locked gates and inappropriate stiles. It's best to shrug your shoulders and remain philosophical, the rest of the route more than rewards the effort.*

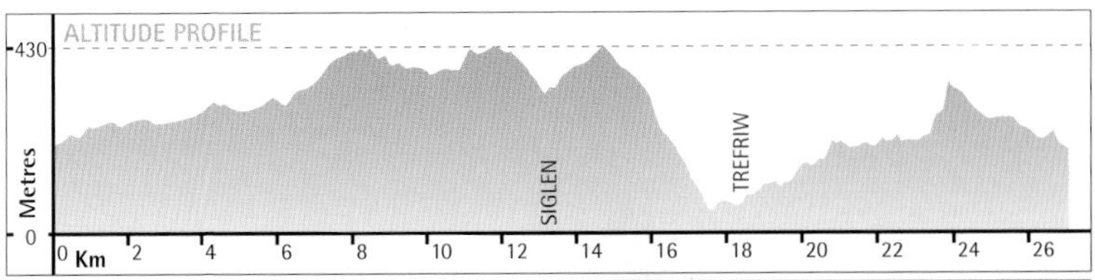

THE CARNEDDAU – SNOWDONIA **GRADE: ▲**

TOTAL DISTANCE: 27KM » **TOTAL ASCENT**: 940M » **TIME**: 3-4 HOURS » **START/FINISH**: CAPEL CURIG
START GRID REF: SH 720582 » **SATNAV**: LL24 0EN » **OS MAP**: EXPLORER OL17; LANDRANGER 115
PUB: BRYN TYRCH, CAPEL CURIG, TEL: 01690 720 223 » **CAFÉ**: LAKESIDE, LLYN CRAFNANT, TEL: 01492 640 818; CAFFI SIABOD, CAPEL CURIG TEL: 01690 720 429

Hafod-y-
rhiw
Eilio
1064
Cairn
Penywaun-
wen
Craig yr
Ysfa
Cwm
Eigiau
64
Settlement
Cedryn
Garreg
5
833
Pen yr Helgi Du
63
Ffynnon
Llugwy Resr
Bwlch y
Tri Marchog
Pen Llithrig
y Wrach
799
Llyn Cowlyd Reservoir
30m
10m
634
Creigiau Gleision
Carreg Mianog
62
Afon Llugwy
678
Glan Llugwy
61
Cairn
4
Settlement
3
Rhyd-goch
69
71
72
73
2
Tal-y-braich
548
Craig Wen
Blaen-y-
MS
267
Helyg
Gŵf
Isaf
60
A5
264
Nant yr Ogof
Afon Llugwy
MS
Tal-y-waun
Crimpiau
Gallt yr Ogof
Nant y Gors
59
Bron Heulog
763
MS
Ardincaple
Gelli
460
P
S
Clogwyn-
mawr
441
Cefn y Capel
MS
Capel Curig
PH
Plas Curig
186
195
Plas y Brenin
National Mountain
Centre
Cairn
Hotel
Mymbyr
A 4086
MS
Hotel
Dyffryn
193

19 THE CARNEDDAU – SNOWDONIA

Directions – The Carneddau – Snowdonia

S Turn **R** out of the car park, onto a tarmac track that soon becomes rough. Continue for 4.5km, and then, after passing the Gwern Gof Isaf campsite, bear **R**, over a bridge, to the A5. Turn **R** for 600m and bear **L** onto a track (waymarked as footpath but actually a bridleway).

2 Follow this track past one house, towards a second, and go through a gate and then turn **L** directly uphill towards a marker post (no path). Follow this up to a gate; go through and then turn **R** to follow singletrack around the hillside to a junction with a good track. Bear **R** for a few metres, and then **L**, immediately ahead of the wall, to drop on a stony track to a gate and footbridge.

3 Cross the bridge and bear **L** to follow a faint and boggy path that soon establishes itself and climbs steeply up the hillside to a gate next to a leat (watercourse). The actual line of the bridleway is impossible to follow here so best to bear **R**, alongside the leat, and continue past one bridge to a second, where you turn **L** to ride through heather to a stile. Cross this and turn **R** to follow singletrack down into a saddle above the lake.

4 Aim **L** of the reservoir and the vague grassy track quickly becomes technical singletrack, which you follow all the way towards the far end. As the good stuff ends, look to fork **L** and climb the bank to stay on the exact line of the bridleway. This leads to a fork, where you keep **SA**. (If you miss the **L** fork and arrive by the dam next to a building, bear **L** to climb zigzags to the junction and turn **R**.)

5 Follow the track down past a derelict house and beneath the pipeline. Keep **SA** to climb steeply, and then descend, equally as steeply (sorry!), into Trefriw. Bear **R** at the T-junction, and climb easily up to Llyn Crafnant.

6 Follow the road along the lakeside and past the café and at the end, go through a gate and climb **SA** on a gravel drive to a yard. Turn **L** on a grassy track that leads to a gate. Go through and turn **R** to climb steeply up to a pass and then keep **SA** to descend all the way back to Capel Curig, keeping **R** over a bridge, and following the main track the whole way.

Pronounciation: **Capel Curig** – **Ka-pel Ki-rig**. **Carneddau** – **Kar-neth-eye**.

Making a weekend of it

Snowdon (page 127) is the obvious partner ride to this one, and would make a big weekend. But you could relax afterwards and hook up with either the Marin Trail at Gwydyr Forest near Betws-y-Coed, or nip over to Penmachno.

SINGLETRACK ALONGSIDE LLYN COWLYD RESERVOIR

WONDERFUL CLWYDIAN SINGLETRACK ON THE FLANKS OF MOEL FAMAU

20 The Clwydian Hills – Vale of Clwyd 20km

Introduction

The Clwydian Hills, or plain Clwyds as they are often known, form a whaleback spine that runs through the heart of north-east Wales, rising up in the south, close to Llangollen and the Berwyn Hills, and dipping its toes in the Dee Estuary among the holiday parks of Rhyl and Prestatyn. The hills themselves act as a lofty, heather-covered divide between the lush Vale of Clwyd and the more densely populated estuary of the River Dee. The highpoint, Moel Famau, rises to a respectable 554m above sea level, and although there are no legal trails to the very top, there's plenty to go at on the northern and western flanks, as this route demonstrates nicely.

The Ride

Many loops can be carved out of the Clwydians, but for real quality, and the chance to sample the best trails in the area, this 20km loop is hard to beat. It starts close to the tiny village of Cilcain, to the north of Moel Famau, and, after a brief traverse, which offers great singletrack as well as a short section of 'North Shore', it climbs steeply onto the mountain's northern slopes. Broad grassy tracks give way to sinuous moorland singletrack, courtesy of some seriously good permissive bridleways, and after great views across the valley to Moel Dywyll, it clambers onto the north-east ridge and the ride's highpoint. The descent follows a great grassy doubletrack that's frighteningly fast – watch out for walkers on their way up – before more permissive bridleway traverses the hillside to Llangynhafal; a possible lunch stop. The return leg follows road and track around Moel Llys-y-coed, and after looping nearly the whole way around the mountain, singletrack takes over to drop to the reservoir at Garth.

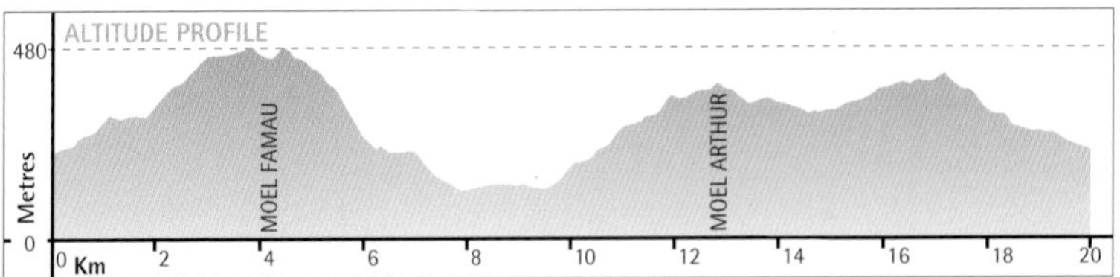

THE CLWYDIAN HILLS – VALE OF CLWYD **GRADE: ▲**

TOTAL DISTANCE: 20KM » **TOTAL ASCENT**: 710M » **TIME**: 2.5-4 HOURS » **START/FINISH**: CILCAIN, NR THE PUMPHOUSE **START GRID REF**: SJ 171647 » **SATNAV**: CH7 5PF » **OS MAP**: EXPLORER 265; LANDRANGER 116 » **PUB**: THE GOLDEN LION, LLANGYNHAFAL, TEL 01824 790 451; THE WHITE HORSE INN, CILCAIN, TEL: 01352 740 142; THE WE THREE, LOGGERHEADS, TEL: 01352 810 337 » **CAFÉ**: LOGGERHEADS COUNTRY PARK, TEL: 01352 810 397

DROPPING FROM MOEL FAMAU ON A PERMISSIVE BRIDLEWAY

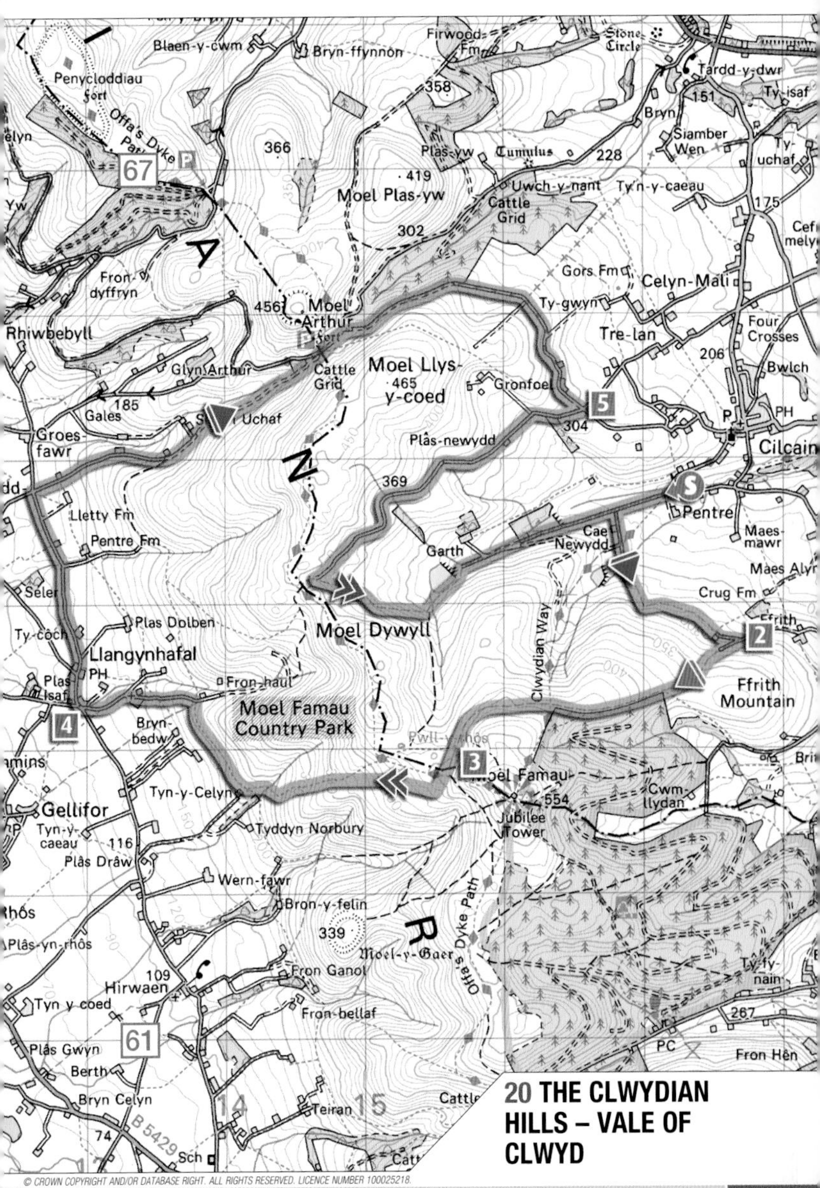

20 THE CLWYDIAN HILLS – VALE OF CLWYD

Directions – The Clwydian Hills – Vale of Clwyd

S Ride uphill from the car park and continue to a T-junction. Turn **L** here onto another broad track. Follow this around the hillside and keep **SA** as it becomes singletrack and crosses a short section of boardwalk. Continue to a junction with a clear track that merges in from the right (marked with a fingerpost).

2 Turn **sharp R** here (signed *Moel Famau*) and climb steeply up out of the wood and on through a gate. Keep **SA** to another gate and now continue, with walls on both sides, to another gate that leads out onto open ground. Keep **SA** onto singletrack (permissive bridleway) and stay with this as it climbs and drops a few times before eventually going through a gate on the top of the ridge. Keep ahead for 5m to a crossroads with the main track up onto Moel Famau.

3 Keep **SA** to descend on grassy doubletrack and stay with this (permissive bridleway) to the bottom, where you turn **R** onto a traversing track that drops to cross a stream and then climbs out again. Keep **SA**, along the foot of open ground, until a gate leads onto a track that drops to a road. Bear **L**. Drop to a crossroads and turn **R** into Llangynhafal.

4 Continue past The Golden Lion and keep **SA** for another 1km to a crossroads. Turn **R** and climb to a gate, where you continue on a gravel track to the road at the pass beneath Moel Arthur. Turn **R** onto the road and then **R** again, onto a broad track that leads through a gate and around the hillside. Continue onto a surfaced road and drop to a crossroads, where you turn **R**.

5 This now deteriorates into a rough track that traverses the hillside and climbs easily back towards the top of the ridge. Look for a waymarker post on the left and turn **L** (signed *Cilcain*) to enjoy a singletrack descent to a stream crossing. Cross the stream and bear **L** to continue on singletrack to a gate that leads onto a rough track. Turn **R** onto this and follow it easily back to the car park.

Moel means 'bare or rounded' hilltop. There are plenty of these in the Clwydian Range.

Making a day of it

It's possible to loop northwards from the Moel Arthur car park or, alternatively, link up with forest tracks south of Moel Famau and link these with the Loggerheads Country Park.

Making a weekend of it

The best bet is the trail centre at Coed Llandegla, where there's plenty to go at. Another alternative would be to link this one in with the **Berwyn Hills** route (page 119) further south.

SECTION 4

Bonus Section

Only a few miles over the border in England, the whaleback ridge of Long Mynd is undoubtedly Welsh in character, and this circuit, starting in Church Stretton, makes the best of it, including the renowned singletrack of Minton Batch.

LONG MYND RIDING, SHROPSHIRE

MINTON BATCH SINGLETRACK

MINTON BATCH SINGLETRACK

21 **The Long Mynd** – Shropshire 32km

Introduction

The Long Mynd forms a lofty whaleback ridge that towers above the tiny Shropshire Town of Church Stretton, just a few miles from the Wales/ England border. It's undoubtedly English in position, but it's definitely more Welsh in nature, rising to a respectable 516m at its highest point, Pole Bank, and concealing some absolutely top-notch riding; including Minton Batch – one of the finest stretches of 'natural' singletrack in the country. And there's also a definite connection with the principality: Mynd is thought to be an anglicised abbreviation of the Welsh 'mynydd' which means mountain. It's an appropriate moniker; the Long Mynd is exactly that – a long mountain.

The Ride

The Mynd is a compact ridge really, so any attempt to squeeze 30km out of it is going to involve climbing and dropping a few times from its lofty top. Fortunately the climbs are mainly rideable, despite being steep in places, especially in the middle stages of Carding Mill Valley; and the descents are absolutely sumptuous, with the sinuous singletrack down Minton Batch as good as anything in the book, calling for a cool head and a tightrope walker's balance in places as the chasm to the right gets deeper and more worrying. The cruisy sections along the top are also excellent, and offer plenty of opportunity to enjoy the huge views in all directions.

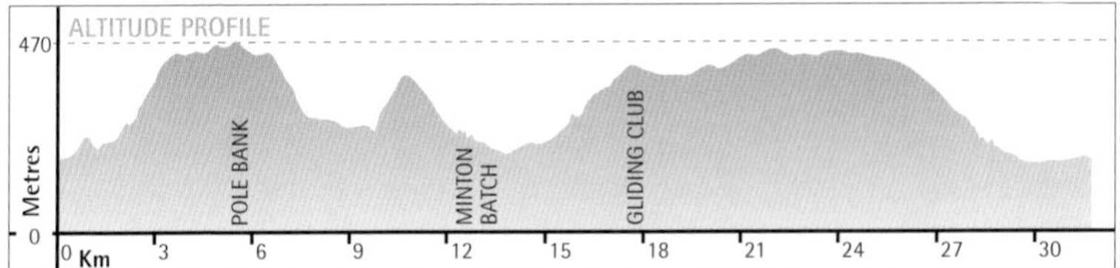

THE LONG MYND **GRADE: ▲**

TOTAL DISTANCE: 32KM » **TOTAL ASCENT**: 1,100M » **TIME**: 3.5-5 HOURS » **START/FINISH**: CHURCH STRETTON, CO-OP CAR PARK
START GRID REF: SO 453935 » **SATNAV**: SY6 6BX » **OS MAP**: EXPLORER 217; LANDRANGER 137 » **PUB**: THE YEW TREE INN, ALL STRETTON, TEL: 01694 722 228; LOTS OF CHOICE IN CHURCH STRETTON » **CAFÉ**: LOTS IN CHURCH STRETTON

Asterton
Prolley Moor
Mytton Way
Shropshire Way
Myndtown
Black Knoll
Handless
Hillend Fm
River Onny
Churchmoor Hill
Churchmoor Rough
Churchmoor Hall
Gliding Club
Synalds
Tumulus
Tumuli
Knolls
Minton Batch
Yapsel Bank
Callow Hollow
Packetstone Hill
Packet Stone
Priors Holt Hill
Priors Holt
Pillocksgreen
Woolston
Brokenstones
Blakemoor
Cwm Head
Hamperley
Shooter's Knoll
Minton
Callow
Little Stretton
Hotel
Waterfall
Manor Fm
Motts
New Ho
Marshbrook
Whittingslow
ROMAN ROAD (course of)
Bushmoor
The Corner
Wettles
Felhampton
Marsh Fm
Swiss Cott
Oakwood
Acton Scott
Hall
Working Farm
Henley
Henley Common
Wolvert
Ireland
Manor Fm
The Hough
Raggdon
Ragleth Hill
Dryhill Fm
Jack Mytton Way

BONUS ROUTE – THE LONG MYND

Directions – The Long Mynd – Shropshire

S Keep the Co-op to your left and ride up to the main road. Turn **R** and then first **L** (*Burway Rd*). Keep **R** at a junction and then keep **L** at the next fork (dead end right) to climb for 500m to a cattle grid. Turn **R** here onto a broad track and follow it down into Carding Mill Valley. Keep **SA**, past the Pavilion, and stay on the main track that climbs up the valley floor. Bear **R** where a footpath goes left up a tributary valley, and continue to the very top, where you'll meet a good track.

2 Turn **L** onto this and follow it to a fork, where you go **R** onto a waymarked bridleway. Continue **SA** over a road and climb to Pole Bank. Descend the other side and turn **R** onto the road. Pass an enclosure on the right and then turn immediately **R** onto a broad track (signed *Stanbatch*).

3 Follow this through the heather and descend steeply to the road. Turn **L** and keep **SA** when another road joins from the right. Continue **SA** onto a rough track that contours around the hillside to eventually join a road.

4 Turn **L** to climb steeply up past the Glider Club viewing area to the Glider Club entrance. Turn **L** until you pass the fenced off area to your left and then turn **R** onto a grassy trail that crosses a heathery plateau before ducking into the obvious notch of Minton Batch.

5 Stay with the trail as it narrows and provides a stunning singletrack descent. Keep **SA** the whole time, eventually passing a farm on the other side of the stream and then crossing the stream to drop to a road.

6 Turn **R** and continue to a T-junction where you turn **R** again (signed *Churchmoor*). Follow the road up to a three-way junction and take the middle track that climbs steeply up into a plantation. Keep **SA** on the main track and **ignore** a good track off left early on and then another, to the right, a bit later. Climb to a track crossroads and turn **R** to the forest edge, where you keep **SA** to a gate.

7 Go through this and follow waymarks over the hilltop to a broad track. Turn **R** onto this and follow it out of the Glider Club and past Minton Batch. Keep ahead on the road, passing the earlier descent to Stanbatch on your left, and then, with Pole Bank ahead. Stay on the road to traverse around the foot of the hill to a T-junction.

8 Bear **sharp L** and continue around Pole Bank to the track you took earlier. Bear **R** onto this and then **L** at a fork to continue past the top of Carding Mill Valley to another fork, where you keep **L** to the road. Turn **R** onto this and then, immediately before a cattlegrid, turn **R** onto a waymarked Bridleway **(note: marked footpath on the OS map)**.

9 Follow this along the edge of the open ground and fork **R** onto a broad muddy track that then drops to a junction and marker pole by a wall and a house. Bear **half R** and follow another marker down a steep ramp. Bear **R** to follow the bridleway signs around the hillside **(note: this trail isn't marked on the map)** and drop to the valley floor, where you turn **sharp L** to drop all the way down to All Stretton. Turn **R** back to Church Stretton.

Making a day of it

This route really utilises all the best bits of the Mynd, but, for the really energetic, there is an opportunity to head west towards Stiperstones, using a variety of decent bridleways and narrow lanes.

THE FINAL DROP TO ALL STRETTON

Appendix

Tourist Information Centres

South Wales

Abergavenny T: 01873 853 254
Brecon T: 01874 622 485
Brecon Beacons National Park T: 01874 623 366
Llandovery T: 01550 720 693
Newport (Dyfed) T: 01239 820 912
Swansea T: 01792 468 321

Mid Wales

Knighton T: 01547 528 753
Llanidloes T: 01686 412 287
Machynlleth T: 01654 761 244
Presteigne T: 01544 260 650
Rhayader T: 01597 810 898

North Wales

Barmouth T: 01341 280 787
Betws-y-Coed T: 01690 710 426
Dolgellau T: 01341 422 888
Harlech T: 01766 780 658
Llanberis T: 01286 870 765
Llangollen T: 01978 860 828
Mold T: 01352 759 331

Weather

www.metoffice.gov.uk – Specific mountain forecasts for Snowdonia and the Brecon Beacons
www.metcheck.com

Food and Drink

Cafés

South Wales

Trading Post, Abergavenny T: 01873 855 448
No 18, Crickhowell T: 01873 811 000
Bridge Café, Brecon T: 01874 622 024
The Bay Bistro, Rhosili T: 01792 390 519
Fronlas Café, Newport T: 01239 820 351

Mid Wales

Drovers Restaurant,
Llanwrtyd Wells T: 01591 610 264
Elan Valley Visitor Centre Cafe T: 01597 810 899
Strand Café, Rhayader T: 01982 552 652
Cwmddeudwr Arms, Rhayader T: 01597 811 343

North Wales

Pete's Eats, Llanberis T: 01286 870 117
Caffi Siabod, Capel Curig T: 01690 720 429
Lakeside Restaurant,
Llyn Crafnant T: 01492 640 818
Caffi Florence,
Loggerheads Country Park T: 01352 810 397

Pubs

South Wales

Dragon's Head,
Llangenny (nr Crickhowell) T: 01873 810 350
Hen & Chicken, Abergavenny T: 01873 853 613
The Bear Hotel, Crickhowell T: 01873 810 408
The Dragons Back,
Pengenfford T: 01874 711 353
The Castle Inn, Llangorse T: 01874 658 225
The New Inn, Ystradfellte T: 01639 720 211
The King's Head, Llangennith T: 01792 386 212
Llwyngwair Arms, Newport T: 01239 820 267

Mid Wales

Nueadd Arms, Llanwrtyd Wells T: 01591 610 236
Crown Inn, Rhayader T: 01597 811 099
Severn Stars Inn, Aberedu T: 01982 560 494
Radnor Arms, New Radnor T: 01544 350 232
Towy Bridge Inn,
Rhandirmwyn T: 01550 760 370
Royal Oak, Rhandirmwyn T: 01550 760 201
The Star Inn, Dylife T: 01650 521 345

North Wales

The George III Hotel,
Penmaenpool T: 01341 422 525
Ysgethin Inn, Talybont T: 01341 247 578
The West Arms,
Llanarmon Dyffryn Ceiriog T: 01691 600 665
The Bryn Tyrch, Capel Curig T: 01690 720 223
The Cwellyn Arms, Rhyd Ddu T: 01766 890 321
The Heights, Llanberis T: 01286 238 235
The We Three Loggerheads,
Loggerheads T: 01352 810 337
The White Horse Inn, Cilcain T: 01352 740 142

Accommodation YHA

South Wales

Llangattock T: 01873 812 307
Llwyn y Celyn, Brecon T: 0845 371 9029
Danywenallt,
Talybont-on-Usk T: 0845 371 9548
Port Eynon T: 0845 371 9135
Newport T: 0845 371 9543

Mid Wales

Tyncornel (Independent) T: 01980 629 259

North Wales

Kings, Dolgellau T: 0845 371 9327
Betws-y-Coed T: 01690 710 796
Snowdon Ranger T: 0845 371 9659
Llanberis T: 0845 371 9645
Idwal Cottage T: 0845 371 9744
For other options visit **www.yha.org.uk**

Camping

Below are a few sites that are well positioned for some of the routes. For others contact the local Tourist Information Centre, or try **www.ukcampsite.co.uk**

South Wales

Pyscodlyn, Abergavenny T: 01873 853 271
Gilestone, Talybont-on-Usk T: 01874 676 236
Llangorse Lake T: 01874 658 226
The Dragons Back,
Pengenfford T: 01874 711 353
Three Cliffs Bay, Gower T: 01792 371 218
Hendre Farm, Newport T: 01239 820 208

Mid Wales

Towy Bridge, Rhandirmwyn,
(no booking required) T: 01550 760 370
Gigrin Farm, Rhayader T: 01597 810 243

North Wales

Bryn Tyrch Farm, Capel Curig T: 01690 720 414
Cwellyn Arms, Rhyd Ddu T: 01766 890 321
Fron Farm, Mold T: 01352 741 482
Y Giler Arms,
Nr Betws-y-Coed T: 01690 770 612

Hotels and Pub B&B

South Wales

The Bear Hotel, Crickhowell T: 01873 810 408
The Castle Inn, Pengenfford T: 01874 711 353
The Traveller's Rest,
Talybont-on-Usk T: 01874 676 233
The King's Head, Llangennith T: 01792 386 212

Mid Wales

Nueadd Arms, Llanwrtyd Wells T: 01591 610 236
Royal Oak, Rhandirmwyn T: 01550 760 201
Crown Inn, Rhayader T: 01597 811 099

North Wales

The George III Hotel,
Penmaenpool T: 01341 422 525
The West Arms,
Llanarmon Dyffryn Ceiriog T: 01691 600 665
The Bryn Tyrch, Capel Curig T: 01690 720 223
The Cwellyn Arms, Rhyd Ddu T: 01766 890 321
Dolafon Guest House T: 01286 870 993

Bike Shops

South Wales

Gateway Cycles, Abergavenny
T: 01873 858 519 .... www.gatewaycycles.co.uk

Biped Cycles, Brecon
T: 01874 622 296 .... www.bipedcycles.co.uk

Skyline Cycles, Afan
T: 01639 850 011 .... www.skylinecycles.co.uk

Afan Valley Bike Shed
T: 01639 851 406 ... www.afanvalleybikeshed.co.uk

Mid Wales

Clive Powell, Rhayader
T: 01597 811 343 ...... www.clivepowell-mtb.co.uk

Summit Cycles, Aberystwyth
T: 01970 626 061 .... www.summitcycles.co.uk

North Wales

Beics Brenin, Coed y Brenin
T: 01341 440 728 .... www.beicsbrenin.co.uk

Dolgellau Cycles
T: 01341 423 332 .... www.dolgellaucycles.co.uk

Framed Bicycle Company, Llanberis
T: 01286 871 188 ... www.theframedbicycleco.com

Bike Hire

Biped Cycles, Brecon .... T: 01874 622 296
Beics Brenin, Coed y Brenin ... T: 01341 440 728
Clive Powell, Rhayader .... T: 01597 811 343
Beics Betws, Betws-y-coed ..... T: 01690 710 766

MTB Holidays/Weekends

Tom Hutton MTB Guiding,
Snowdonia .... T: 07974 912 479
www.mtbguiding.co.uk

Clive Powell, Rhayader .... T: 01597 811 343
www.clivepowell-mtb.co.uk

Other Contacts

www.mbwales.com

Other Publications

Mountain Biking Trail Centres – The Guide
Tom Fenton, Vertebrate Publishing
www.v-publishing.co.uk

Great Britain Mountain Biking – The Best Trail Riding in England, Scotland and Wales
Tom Fenton & Andy McCandlish, Vertebrate Publishing
www.v-publishing.co.uk

The Author

It took Tom over 20 years to realise that he didn't look good in a suit and tie, and less than five minutes to resign from his day job to concentrate on writing and photography and later guiding. He's since won awards for his words and pictures and travelled extensively throughout the UK and abroad. He has been mountain biking since the sport's inception, and as a natural explorer with an almost unhealthy fascination with maps, has been instrumental in documenting routes all over the British Isles.

He's best known as the person behind the pull-out routes section in **MBR** (Mountain Bike Rider) Magazine but also contributes to many other outdoor publications, covering everything from climbing to kayaking. He has also written and illustrated a number of guidebooks.

When he's not writing or exploring, he runs a mountain bike guiding/holiday business, MTB Guiding, which offers everything from guided rides and weekend breaks in Snowdonia to full, week-long mountain bike holidays in Wales, the Lake District and Scotland.

He lives on the flanks of Snowdon with his partner, Steph – also a cycling fanatic – and their Labrador, Du.
www.mtbguiding.co.uk

Vertebrate Publishing

Mountain Bike Rider (MBR) Magazine called our MTB guides *'...a series of glossy, highly polished and well researched guidebooks to some of the UK's favourite riding spots.'*

We want to provide you – the rider – with well-researched, informative, functional, inspirational and great-looking MTB guide-books that document the superb riding across the length and breadth of the UK. So if you want to go riding somewhere, you can always count on us to point you in the right direction.

As well as our series of MTB guidebooks, we have award-winning and bestselling titles covering a range of leisure activities, including; cycling, rock climbing, hillwalking and others. We are best known for our MTB titles, including the bestseller *Dark Peak Mountain Biking*, which **BIKEmagic.com** said was *'far and away the best Peak guide we've come across'*.

Our autobiography of the British rock climbing legend **Jerry Moffatt** won the *Grand Prize* at the *2009 Banff Mountain Book Festival*.

We also produce many leading outdoor titles for other publishers including the **Mountain Training UK** (MTUK) and rock climbing guidebooks for the **British Mountaineering Council** and the **Fell and Rock Climbing Club**. For more information, please visit our website: **www.v-publishing.co.uk** or email us: **info@v-publishing.co.uk**

PHOTO: JOHN COEFIELD

MOUNTAIN BIKING GUIDEBOOKS

About the Great Outdoors

The great outdoors is not bottom bracket friendly; beautiful flowing singletrack can give way suddenly to scary rock gardens, hard climbs can appear right at the end of a ride and sheep will laugh at your attempts to clean your nemesis descent. Of course it's not all good news. You'll need a good bike to ride many of the routes in our set of mountain biking guides. You'll also need fuel, spare clothing, first aid skills, endurance, power, determination and plenty of nerve.

Bridleways litter our great outdoors. Our guides, written by local riders, reveal the secrets of their local area's best rides from 6 to 300km in length, including ideas for link-ups and night-riding options. Critically acclaimed, our comprehensive series of guides is the country's bestselling and most respected – purpose-built for the modern mountain biker.

The Guidebooks

Each guidebook features up to 28 rides, complete with comprehensive directions, specialist mapping and inspiring photography, all in a pocket-sized, portable format. Written by riders for riders, our guides are designed to maximise ride-ability and are full of useful local area information.

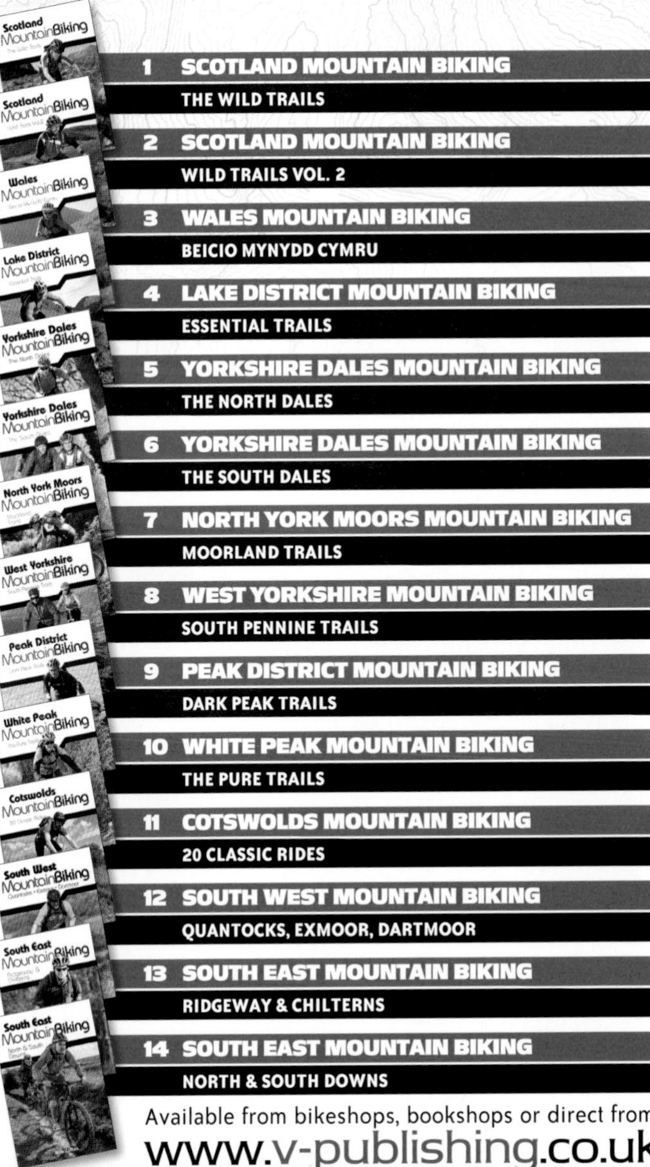
1 SCOTLAND MOUNTAIN BIKING
THE WILD TRAILS
2 SCOTLAND MOUNTAIN BIKING
WILD TRAILS VOL. 2
3 WALES MOUNTAIN BIKING
BEICIO MYNYDD CYMRU
4 LAKE DISTRICT MOUNTAIN BIKING
ESSENTIAL TRAILS
5 YORKSHIRE DALES MOUNTAIN BIKING
THE NORTH DALES
6 YORKSHIRE DALES MOUNTAIN BIKING
THE SOUTH DALES
7 NORTH YORK MOORS MOUNTAIN BIKING
MOORLAND TRAILS
8 WEST YORKSHIRE MOUNTAIN BIKING
SOUTH PENNINE TRAILS
9 PEAK DISTRICT MOUNTAIN BIKING
DARK PEAK TRAILS
10 WHITE PEAK MOUNTAIN BIKING
THE PURE TRAILS
11 COTSWOLDS MOUNTAIN BIKING
20 CLASSIC RIDES
12 SOUTH WEST MOUNTAIN BIKING
QUANTOCKS, EXMOOR, DARTMOOR
13 SOUTH EAST MOUNTAIN BIKING
RIDGEWAY & CHILTERNS
14 SOUTH EAST MOUNTAIN BIKING
NORTH & SOUTH DOWNS
Available from bikeshops, bookshops or direct from:
www.v-publishing.co.uk

ORDER DIRECT FROM
www.v-publishing.co.uk
VP

JEROEN HOEK ENJOYING THE VIEWS ON THE WAY TO THE SUMMIT OF CADAIR IDRIS.